Life's a Drag!
Danny La Rue
& The Drag Scene

Peter Underwood

Life's a Drag!

LESLIE FREWIN OF LONDON

Danny La Rue
& The Drag Scene

By the same author

A Gazetteer of British Ghosts
Into the Occult
Horror Man – The Life and Work of Boris Karloff
A Gazetteer of Scottish and Irish Ghosts
*The Ghost of Borley – A Critical History of 'The Most Haunted House
in England'* (with Dr. Paul Tabori)
A Host of Hauntings
Haunted London

For
Pauline and John Thompson – in friendship

First published 1974 by
Leslie Frewin Publishers Limited,
Five Goodwin's Court,
Saint Martin's Lane,
London WC2N 4LL, England.

Second Impression 1974

This book is printed in Garamond Bold
Photoset, printed and bound in Great Britain by
Weatherby Woolnough, Sanders Road,
Wellingborough, Northamptonshire

ISBN 0 85632 081 1

Contents

List of Illustrations   7

Introduction   9

Part 1   The Man and the Myth   17

Part 2   They All Love Danny   31

Part 3   The Early Years   49

Part 4   The Long Climb to the Top   79

Part 5   The Results of Success   115

Acknowledgements   181

Select Bibliography   185

Index   187

List of Illustrations

Page

Successful Danny La Rue in 1968, the year that he appeared in Summer Season at Margate; had his own television special; took part in the Royal Television Show and saw the release of his first record: *On Mother Kelly's Doorstep. (Photo: Central Press Ltd.)*   24

Young Danny Carroll (upper right) peeling potatoes as a Boy Scout around the camp fire at Trehill, Devon. *(Photo: John R. Waldron)*   25

Young Danny Carroll as a teenage cadet in Devon *(Photo: A. Lukan)*   25

A sketch (Danny in centre) from *Call It a Day* by Dodie Smith. *(Photo: Esmé Cooper)*   62

Danny, extreme right, in the YWCA revue *Call It a Day. (Photo: Esmé Cooper)*   62

A young Daniel Carroll (later Danny La Rue) in the YWCA production of *April Folly. (Photo: Esmé Cooper)*   63

Daniel Carroll (Danny La Rue) in the YWCA production of *April Folly. (Photo: Esmé Cooper)*   63

The full cast of *April Folly* with Danny on the extreme right. *(Photo: Esmé Cooper)*   63

Rare photographs of Danny La Rue backstage as the transformation takes place, 1966. *(Photos: Syndication International)*   64

Danny with Mary Talbot's portrait at the Trafford Galleries, London. April 1967. *(Photo: Keystone)*   65

A photograph by David Steen of Danny in the dressing room of his legendary Hanover Square club. *(Photo: Camera Press)*   94

Danny reproduced every facet of the Bunny Girl mystique in one of his most famous routines at his club. *(Photo: David Steen, Camera Press Ltd.)*   94

Danny with Ronnie Corbett at a rehearsal for the 1969 Royal Variety Show. Ronnie's eye had been injured in a car crash. *(Photo: Syndication International)*   95

Danny masquerades as an English rose for his night-club act. *(Photo: David Steen, Camera Press Ltd.)*   95

A typically lavish pantomime production. Danny with Alan Haynes. *(Photo: Daniel Farson)*   96

Danny (right) as a trendy blonde in a sketch with Alan Haynes, a memorable partnership. *(Photo: Daniel Farson)*   96

Danny as Lady Godiva in the Coventry Theatre Birthday Show, 1969. *(Photo: Keystone)*   96

Page

Larry Grayson: 'I did a drag act for many years, but I never liked those lashes and wigs'. *(Photo: Larry Grayson)*   97

Rex Jameson as the inimitable 'Mrs Shufflewick'. *(Photo: Rex Jameson)*   97

Five famous 'Charlie's Aunts' at the Apollo Theatre, December 1970. Back Row: Philip Dale, Tom Courtenay (the latest Charlie) and Leslie Phillips; front: John Mills and Danny. *(Photo: Syndication International)*   97

Roy Hudd, Lionel Blair and Danny in high spirits during rehearsals for *Danny La Rue at the Palace,* 1970. *(Photo: Keystone)*   146

Danny and the company in the fabulously successful *Danny La Rue at the Palace,* 1970. *(Photo: Tom Hustler, Keystone)*   146

HRH Princess Margaret chats with Danny and other members of the cast backstage at the Palace Theatre, April 8, 1970. *(Photo: Associated Press Ltd.)*   147

Danny and Lord Snowdon enjoy a joke after the premiere of *Danny La Rue at the Palace,* held in aid of the Invalid Children's Aid Association, 1970. *(Photo: Syndication International)*   147

Danny, as Fanny Oakley, with Roy Hudd in *Danny La Rue at the Palace,* 1970. *(Photo: Central Press Photos Ltd.)*   147

Picking up some points on beauty. Danny with Miss World contestants at the Savoy Hotel, November 1970. *(Photo: Central Press Photos Ltd.)*   148

The Variety Club of Great Britain's 1970 Annual Ladies' Luncheon at the Dorchester Hotel. Writer Mary Hayley Bell (right), actor John Mills (left) and a guest chat with Danny. *(Photo: Syndication International)*   148

Danny with a two hundred-year old automatic drum-playing bear after he had opened the Kensington Antiques Fair, October 1971. *(Photo: Keystone)*   148

Danny in SS uniform, enjoys a joke on the set of *Our Miss Fred* with fellow star Lance Percival. *(Photo: Keystone)*   149

Our Miss Fred (1972) Danny's first film, was set in France in the 1940s and Danny wore fifteen different wigs and dyed his own hair for the first time ever for the part of Fred Wimbush who dons SS uniform in parts of the film. *(Photo: Keystone)*   149

July 1970. Danny becomes the owner of The Swan Inn, Streatley and realizes two ambitions: to operate a good country hotel and to own an island. *(Photo: Keystone)*   177

Introduction

FOR SOMETHING LIKE TEN YEARS IT WAS AN UNFORGETTABLE EXPERIENCE TO be among the audience in a crowded theatre in London or the provinces when the music swelled, the curtain rose and there, attired in some breathtakingly beautiful ensemble, stood a glamorous, magnetic, sparkling female figure that attracted every eye: the one and only Danny La Rue.

In 1963 Danny first appeared in his own London show and in November 1973 he announced that he planned to hang up his bra, his gowns and his wigs. Time will show whether he sticks to this decision; but he just might.

'I'm basically a comedian,' he told Vincent Firth of *Film Review*. 'I never even think of myself as a man or as a woman when I'm in drag. I'm just an actor playing a woman. My gowns are the tools of my trade just as costume changes are to Laurence Olivier. My act is playing a woman, knowing that everybody knows it's a fella. That's the point of the joke. If I played a woman's role from beginning to end, where would Danny La Rue have got to?'

What is the significance of the fact that the highest-paid performer on the English stage is a man dressed as a woman? Can this fact be indicative of a decadent society or is it that English audiences, to a greater degree than most, thrive on blue humour? Or is it a tribute to the artistry, subtlety and professionalism of a 'genius' or at any rate a great performer in the classic music hall tradition?

Of his show at the Prince of Wales theatre over Christmas 1973 – when he practically blackmailed his audience into attending by announcing that it would be the last chance to see him in drag – the *Stage* said it was 'good enough to run until he is ready to draw the old age pension.' Robert Cushman in the *Observer* however, found the show monotonous and Danny himself 'merely a competent gag man and a powerful but anonymous vocalist.'

What is the background and the professional career of this man who has given hours of enjoyment to thousands of people; a man who has reached the very top of the entertainment world in a few short years?

Danny La Rue is *almost* an original. His adopted name, out of the ordinary and easily remembered and his female impersonation act, spectacular, polished and professional, are familiar to nine-tenths of the population of Britain, although strangely, he is relatively unknown abroad. Talk of drag and female impersonators anywhere in the British Isles and within a moment the name of Danny La Rue is mentioned, a distinction that applies to very few other entertainers alive today. Charlie Chaplin is synonymous with clowning and knock-about comedy; Bing Crosby with crooning (although some would prefer Frank Sinatra!); Marlene Dietrich perhaps, with the *femme fatale*; but how many more are there of the same calibre?

There are not many show business personalities who have achieved the enviable and lucrative position of being a household name and probably none in so short a time as Danny La Rue who was virtually unknown little more than a decade ago outside the comparatively small *clientèle* of London's top clubs. Today his name is inevitably linked with female impersonation. Whether he likes it or not it seems probable that it is in that context he will be remembered and it is doubtful if even the resourceful, persistent and hard-working Danny will ever succeed in completely disassociating himself from drag and its implications of transvestism and deviation.

When it was first suggested that I should write something of a biography of this complex man who seems to be liked by almost everyone who knows him, I was not over-enthusiastic. His act, so often praised and applauded for its wit, ingenuity and almost uncanny impersonation of females, was not my notion of ideal entertainment.

There is a self-consciousness about his stage appearance that I find jarring. His beautiful costumes, make-up and whole turn-out is a work of art but at the same time it is a front with very little to justify it, once the initial entrance has been made and duly appreciated.

His send-up of famous people is neither a caricature nor a sincere impression; it is a subtle combination of the two, a kind of good-natured take-off that is entertaining to a degree but hardly world-shattering. Yet this man has reached a height hitherto undreamed of by other artistes in this line of entertainment. What *is* it that Danny La Rue has that the others haven't got? I felt that it might be interesting to try to find out.

My search for the real Danny began when I spent the best part of a day with Alec Berg who has known Danny since his very early days as an entertainer; who has worked with him, admired him and, like so many people that I was to meet, considers him head and shoulders above the rest in his particular branch of entertainment and a very nice man into the bargain.

Long ago, when Danny was just starting in show business, someone said to Alec, 'You've got a rival!' and pointed to Danny. Today Alec, living in retirement in Sussex, looks back on many happy years in entertainment and follows Danny's career avidly.

I quickly discovered that my subject was a complex personality; a man who shunned publicity in his private life as much as he courted it publicly, and a man who had erected around himself an almost impenetrable barrier of friends and business associates whose purpose it was to guard and protect him.

That first interview was obtained through my son-in-law, Crispin Derby, and I was very fortunate at such an early stage in reaching someone so close to Danny. I knew at once that the story of this man was something I now wanted to do. I should say here and now that I am anxious not to harm the good relations between Danny and any of his friends and for this reason I shall not always refer to them, or others who have been good enough to take me into their confidence, by name.

My research on Danny La Rue began one summer day at my home in Hampshire; it took me to a pub in Sussex, a hotel in Lancashire, a coastal cottage in North Devon, a sunny garden not far from London Airport, a dressing-room at a country-club, the back rooms of famous and obscure establishments, to theatre restaurants, to night clubs, art galleries, libraries, publishing houses, public and private houses, well-nigh to Dublin and Oslo, and I talked with hundreds of people: actors, entertainers, managers, impresarios, writers, researchers, royalty, friends, fans and rivals of Danny, before I finally returned home, to put together for the first time the Danny La Rue story.

Writing this book has not been easy and I shall always be grateful to those first two people with whom I discussed Danny, Crispin Derby and Alec Berg, for they fired my enthusiasm when they passed on to me not only something of the man's history and personality but also something of the magic and fascination of Danny. I had the feeling that I, like many people, had no idea of what he was really like or how he had succeeded in his professional career and I am hopeful that the result may have an unusual value, perhaps even to Danny himself, for it is Danny as seen through the eyes of other people.

Danny's effectiveness as a performer has a lot to do with his respect for his audience and the fact that he is in reality a very warm, thoughtful and friendly person, without any of the pretensions and hypocrisy often encountered in stage personalities.

This warm and friendly side to him often comes across in his performances as it did at the London Prince of Wales theatre where his show, which I have already referred to, took place around Christmas 1973, a time of lighting restrictions and fuel shortages making travel by train or car difficult, and a time when the London bomb scares were at their height. At the end of the show Danny came forward and thanked everyone for coming, wished them a safe journey home and sent them away happy and glowing with the sheer joy of watching an accomplished speciality performer in what was announced as his last show in female costume.

He did not appear in male attire throughout the entire show although, as always, there were frequent references to his maleness, sometimes crude and often predictable but never really objectionable. Whether or not it does prove to be the last show in which he demonstrates his 'transvestite' skills, the audience gave him a tremendous 'thank you and goodbye'.

In tackling this book I have been fortunate in following up various leads which have always proved interesting and frequently rewarding. Early on my wife heard part of a radio programme in which two sisters, ardent theatregoers, said they were great fans of Danny, and furthermore they made his fancy shirt-fronts. I contacted Alan Melville, who had conducted the interview and although he did not know the address of the ladies concerned, he confirmed that they were indeed great admirers of Danny and he suggested that I might be able to reach them at the theatrical costumiers for whom they worked. The outcome was that I spent several hours with these two ladies and I learned a great deal.

During the course of a *This is Your Life* television programme featuring Larry Grayson, Danny made an appearance and referred to his friendship with Larry and his great admiration for a hard-working and talented performer. I subsequently met Larry and talked for a long time with him about Danny and his world.

A newspaper interview referred to Danny's having acted in some Young Women's Christian Association productions: yes, YWCA! I contacted the General Secretary and obtained some interesting facts about Danny's early acting days and this led me to other people who had known and worked with Danny when he was still known as Daniel Carroll.

These are just three of the many fruitful leads that have resulted in my obtaining background information and little-known facts about Danny La Rue.

There may be gaps to fill in, but I have used the prerogative of a biographer in deciding what to say and what not to say and anyway I have long been of the opinion that the best of most biographies and certainly biographies of living people, lies between the lines.

Peter Underwood

The Savage Club
St James's Street
London SW1
1974

Part One
The Man and
the Myth

DRAG HAS BEEN DEFINED AS 'WOMEN'S CLOTHING WORN BY MEN' (*PENGUIN English Dictionary*) but the drag act is more generally accepted as female clothing worn by men for the purpose of entertainment.

The word 'drag' is said to be derived from the drag of dresses as distinct from the non-drag of trousers. At all events modern drag has come a long way in a short time; from crude pub entertainment spawned as a giggle over a drink and such activities as Drag Queen Contests, to the superb impersonations by versatile performers, and to a great extent Danny La Rue must take the credit for making drag respectable and accepted in a remarkably short space of time. It is surely significant that he made himself respectable and accepted at the same time.

Danny's act in recent years has been described as a stupendous performance and he has been praised for raising female impersonation to an art form. If that seems something of an overstatement there is no denying that Danny has made drag or female impersonation a popular and accepted entertainment for the whole family.

He is still surprised at his own success and never takes it for granted or thinks that it can last for ever; although he counts among his admirers people like Prince Rainier, Princess Grace, King Hussein, Paul Schofield, Charles Chaplin and Henry Cooper, with the late Noel Coward a particular fan.

Women, as a whole, take offence to drag when it is played straight. Danny realised this and, having achieved perfection in make-up and presentation, then proceeded to 'send up' the whole

thing. In doing so he took the stigma out of drag and may even
have killed drag entertainment in the British pubs that have
enjoyed such an enormous success with these acts in recent years,
especially in certain London and North of England pubs; for a
poll taken in mid-1973 revealed that entertainment of any kind in
pubs is the least popular function of these establishments and it
seems likely that the drag scene in public houses has seen its
heyday, perhaps to be replaced by wrestling!

Drag is however certain to continue in clubs and intimate
theatres where the lewd humour so often associated with drag
performances somehow justifies itself. An artiste can be coarse and
pointedly vulgar in drag to a degree that would not otherwise be
acceptable.

The principal topic of many lesser than top-rank drag
entertainers is sex. The performers regard themselves as clowns
and extend and exploit the accepted liberty of clowns to 'talk
dirty' far beyond the limit which would otherwise be accepted in
public. And there is an added dimension for, while it is generally
supposed to be more permissible for men to 'talk dirty' about sex
than for women to do so, that opinion is maintained by the drag
performers but because they appear as women, the jokes seem
more *risqúe.*

The sexual undertone of drag with its implications of
transvestism and homosexuality is never far away from any female
impersonation act and although Danny now says that his act is
completely sexless, as indeed it is in one sense, there is still

curiosity and imagination at work in the audience and it is indisputable that this is one of the attractions of drag to some people.

The usual initial reaction to a routine drag performance is mingled shock and fascination. There is astonishment at the effectiveness of the impersonation; a mixed confusion and admiration at what is, essentially, a taboo act: a man pretending to be a woman.

Laughter at the comedy of the patter comes as relief and release from the tension generated by the performance and often, naturally enough, there is a desire to see other drag acts for drag is completely different from any other type of entertainment and whether it is to one's particular taste or not, it is an experience that should be explored, if only once in a lifetime, since it extends the accepted world of show business.

In talking with a number of drag artistes I found, as other writers have found, that some female impersonators are extraordinarily sensitive to criticism and will go to considerable lengths to avoid any kind of ridicule or disrespect. It is perhaps fortunate that I am basically uncritical of any form of entertainment, only appreciative of a job well done.

It has seemed to me that the audience that is attracted to Danny's shows is uncritical in approach and mature in years. Invariably the fabulous settings, the sparkling scenes (when he is so often ably supported by talented artistes), the down-to-earth humour, are all well received by an audience that knows what to expect and is pleased when it gets it. There are no surprises, but the well-dressed, respectable audience (few under thirty-five and many over fifty) appear to enjoy thoroughly the uncomplicated patter and the glittering spectacle that is a Danny La Rue show.

It is interesting to notice the development of drag entertainment and today many top-rank impersonators have discovered that the art of female impersonation relies on creating as perfect an impersonation as possible and then breaking it completely; thus forcing the audience to realise and accept that it is being performed by a man. In America as in Britain, this is usually achieved by the impressionist interjecting some aside in a deep voice. Danny's famous '*Wotcher, Mates!*' is an example very much to the point and such skilled performers can create the illusion, break it and then pick it up again, repeatedly; producing tension and release of tension that can be dramatic in the extreme and often very funny, especially when it is done with skill, timing and the perfection born of experience.

The American impersonator Lynne Carter, for example, has been known to do impressions of Hildegarde, Hermione Gingold, Phyllis Diller, Mae West, Bette Davis, Marlene Dietrich and Pearl Bailey, all with a finesse and polish that is almost incredible and all in the space of one hour on one set.

Many straight and normal people seem to like to see their sexual desires ridiculed by drag artistes for, when fun is poked at them, the audience has the satisfaction of knowing that they are not really like the performers. From the drag artistes' point of view many of them (Danny is an exception) for a few hours, are able to be what they would really like to be.

On the other hand many entertainers, especially television performers, have taken to including drag spots in their shows. Dick Emery, Benny Hill and Stanley Baxter come immediately to mind but theirs are usually brief visual cameos incorporated in an otherwise straight comedy show and if any of these artistes, talented as they are, were to do his drag act in a good drag pub, the reception would probably be hostile. It is interesting, to say the least, to know that Danny has never seen a pub drag act.

Benny Hill's character 'Primrose Hill' was an early exercise in drag; rarely used now that others have copied the basic idea. When I asked Benny about his drag performances, he reminded me that drag plays a very small part in his shows and he added: 'I usually do older women, though a fat "Esther O'Gamin" is always funny – to me anyway;' while Dick Emery, after making a considerable hit with his female 'hopefuls': ' . . . Oh! you are awful, but I like you' and 'If you'll forgive the expression . . . ' now uses drag sparingly and concentrates on various and often hilarious male characters.

Danny too has expressed his desire to turn to other things. He admitted to Russell Miller in 1970 that there was nothing he would like better than never to dress as a female again; but it may be that that day is a long way off. He has achieved remarkable success with his painstaking characterisations, considerable fame and fortune and a large and loyal following.

All this will make it difficult for him to turn his back on drag and perform male parts in comedies and perhaps even the occasional straight part. It is a pity in a way for he is quite a good actor, he has 'presence' and a sense of timing, but his name is so firmly associated with female impersonation that his audience will anticipate female impersonation, whether it is there or not, for a long time to come. And perhaps as much as a shoemaker should stick to his last, a drag artiste should stick to drag. Not that Danny can complain about the financial side when he can command a fee of forty thousand pounds for three weeks work, as he did in October 1973 at Batley Variety Club.

Danny is quoted as saying at the time, at Blackpool: 'If an artiste wants big money he's got to come north. London theatres and cabaret rooms just can't compete. You get three times as much money in northern clubs.' His fee, although the highest ever paid to a cabaret artiste in Britain, was dwarfed by the offer of seventy thousand pounds for a week's work at Blighty's Club, Farnworth, that Gerry Slinger, the managing director, made in an effort to attract Frank Sinatra after Slinger heard that the American singer was coming out of retirement towards the end of 1973. Later, Gerry Slinger told me, the offer was increased to a hundred thousand pounds plus expenses.

It seems to me that some drag artistes are almost twin personalities and very mixed-up people. Sir Laurence Olivier, describing his experiences of working with Marilyn Monroe on the film *The Prince and the Showgirl* seems to have found a

Successful Danny La Rue in 1968, the year that he appeared in Summer Season at Margate; had his own television special; took part in the Royal Television Show and saw the release of his first record: *On Mother Kelly's Doorstep*.

Above: Young Danny Carroll (upper right) peeling potatoes as a Boy Scout around the camp fire at Trehill, Devon.

Right: Young Danny Carroll as a teenage cadet in Devon

similar problem. He referred to her as a very difficult girl . . .
almost a twin personality. She seemed to have a deep-seated
resistance to being an actress but had no resistance to being a
show person, a star, or a model. Yet there did seem to be
something about acting that innately frightened her and I have
discovered that this problem is often triggered by an unfortunate
personal experience. Such people 'get their own back' on females
(if they are male) by showing that they can be just as beautiful,
just as graceful, as gentle and as attractive. It is all done quite
unconsciously but there is often a firm reluctance to have any real
and close association with members of the opposite sex, except
perhaps with mother or father or a sister or brother. There is a
craving for the admiration of the female sex (in the case of the
male): girls, ladies of mature years, any female; but the profound
resistance in the personality comes to the fore as soon as there is
any attempt at a close association. This is certainly not the case
with Danny La Rue, an open, normal show biz extrovert of the
best kind.

Just how convincing even an amateur can be in drag was
illustrated in 1970 when a Beauty Queen contest run by a firm in
Norwich was won by a fifteen-year-old boy, Victor Kellor. Some
of the women staff persuaded him to enter the competition and
made a good job of making him up and dressing him in a
mini-dress, wig and well-padded bra. After the hoax was exposed
the girl who came second was declared to be the winner. BBC
disc jockey Terry Wogan was one of the judges and he said

afterwards: 'He was a very convincing girl . . . and I felt he deserved a prize for dressing up so well!' Has Victor found his *forté*, I wonder?

When Danny La Rue arrived in pantomime in London's West End in 1968 he was hailed as a show business genius. A man who, with an exaggerated flutter of eyelashes, a modest foam-rubber bosom and an elaborate coiffure, became the biggest box office draw in London.

There were then and still are those who believe that Danny's act is the result of a decadent society; that it is distasteful and vulgar, even when it is not blue (and his act can at times be the bluest in Britain). Others regard his undoubted artistry, professionalism and occasional subtlety, as the performance of a great entertainer in true music hall tradition.

Danny is popular in his profession and he is generous. Many people find him friendly and helpful; others have been surprised when they have met him and believe that he is a disappointed man.

He is a good conversationalist with an easy and friendly manner, giving the impression that there is no side to him, no falseness; it is an impression that is shared by his friends, by the people who work with him – stars in their own right or stage hands – in fact by almost everyone who meets him.

There are however, several sides to him and it is not always easy to accept everything he says. He feels that honesty is a terribly important quality and said, in at least one interview: 'I always speak the truth.' No matter how small or insignificant the item may be, he says he would hate to be found out telling an untruth.

He stresses again and again that his humour is wholesome and that there is a basic masculinity in his act. He is astute in business matters and the name Danny La Rue is registered under the Business Names Act and also under the Companies Act. The company was initially registered in 1964 with limited liability but re-registered in 1969 as unlimited. It is a shell company and only two shares were issued, one being owned by Danny and the other by his manager, Jack Hanson.

Yet Danny often appears to be naïve and even shortsighted, as when he told Barry Cryer the television and stage writer and actor, that he felt any biography of him 'had an air of obituary'.

For years Danny has been surrounded and sheltered by a close circle of friends and business associates and many people in and out of show business feel that he has to a certain extent lost touch with the general public and that he now exists in a world that is largely of his own making. Many people feel too that he suffers, increasingly, from over-exposure. More than one interviewer has found Danny to be a very different person off-stage; friendly but serious. Sometimes he takes himself very seriously indeed and there are few jokes, if any. Yet, without doubt the female impersonation acts, for which his name has become a household word, have brought him considerable wealth.

At least one experienced drag artiste admitted to me that the female impersonator is often in reality a sad person for while he desperately wants to 'belong' and be a part of society, he has, to a degree, set himself apart since there can be no such person in an ordered community. It has never been an accepted way of life; a 'nice' way of making a living and deep down many, perhaps even most, female impersonators, particularly the more intelligent ones, are morose.

One of Danny's ambitions is to do a character part at the National Theatre. Like most comics he'd love to be thought of as an artiste who can tackle any part. He fancies the role of the Jester in *King Lear* and said, unashamedly, to Sydney Edwards of the London *Evening Standard* in December 1968, 'I want to be a straight actor.'

Another of his aims is to present shows and direct musicals and in fact he was invited to direct a British production of *Lady Be Good.* He was pleased to be asked but said it was impossible. He would like to take on that kind of thing when the public don't want him any more as a performer and being an unwanted performer is a very real fear for Danny. He's always dreaded the day when people would say, in effect, isn't it a shame that he's still going on.

Age brings many problems but to the glamorous female impersonator it presents almost insuperable difficulties for the truly beautiful glamour 'girl' must be young. Age (which is anything over forty) forces the glamour impersonator to turn to comic female impersonation, straight (legitimate) theatre – maybe light comedy, leave the boards and concentrate on management or some behind-the-scenes executive position, or retire gracefully. It is a problem that few have solved satisfactorily but Danny may well find the answer for he is a very practical person, a great one for thrashing things out. If something goes wrong or someone is upset, he thinks nothing of sitting up until the early hours to find a solution to the problem or to ensure that whatever went wrong does not do so again.

Meanwhile Danny continued with the acts that he could do better and with more polish than anyone else and only occasionally did the observant watcher catch a glimpse of the man behind the woman on the stage. Perhaps it was all wearing a bit thin, but there is no doubt that they all love Danny.

Part Two
They All Love Danny

IN OCTOBER 1972 I WENT TO ONE OF THE MOST FAMOUS THEATRICAL
costumiers in the world, Nathans, then in Drury Lane, and there I
talked with two interesting and remarkable ladies.

Passing up the famous stairs that have been climbed by
practically every well-known actor and actress for the last century
and more, signed portraits hang on the walls of the stairs and are
displayed in the upper room, bearing witness to the diversity of
the costumes supplied and the satisfaction of the customers.

Making my way between row upon row of dresses, coats, cloaks
and suits of every description and period, I reached a corner of
the famous establishment where two charming and very elegant
sisters have sat, day after day, sewing sequins, beads, buttons and
lace, stitching ruffles and bows and working magic with their
nimble fingers.

Twins of mature years Violet and Gladys Bennett worked at
Vivian Van Damm's Windmill Theatre, the non-stop variety
showhouse that earned the tag 'We Never Closed' when it became
the only theatre to remain open during the whole of the London
blitz. During its thirty-two years the tiny Windmill theatre
became a Piccadilly landmark; its fame worldwide; a legend in its
lifetime. The non-stop variety show *Revaudeville* had a staggering
run of sixty thousand performances, by far the longest in theatrical
history. Opened in 1932, the theatre finally closed its doors in
1964, to be re-opened as a cinema. Now there is talk of its
becoming a theatre again. After six years at the Windmill during
their early twenties the Bennett sisters continued dressmaking for

the theatre at Bermans; and in fact they have been dressmaking on and off for fifty years.

I gently suggested that they could not have had very much dressmaking to do at the Windmill, as after all it was famous for its nudes. 'That's what we could never understand,' said Gladys. 'You see people said that the Windmill girls never wore any clothes, but it was only a few who didn't; the majority of them had the most lovely gowns. On Monday mornings, after the parade of the Sunday show, Van Damm would come up with one of the young ladies who wore, perhaps, two wheels of white cord on the bosom, just caught together with one piece of cord and he'd say: "What would happen if this cord was to be cut?" The girl would reply, "Well, if you cut it, it would fall apart." Then he'd say, "Well, let's try." And he would cut it. "There, that's what I want", he'd laugh. What he didn't know was that I'd put a piece of very fine pink elastic across it, so that it didn't fall too low!'

Gladys and Violet Bennett related this incident during the course of a broadcast with Alan Melville who commented: 'Oh! I thought that was against the rules at the Windmill?' to which Violet replied: 'It was supposed to be,' and Gladys added, 'Yes, it was supposed to be but that was what happened!'

Danny La Rue is *the* great favourite of the Bennett sisters but Alan Melville worked with another favourite of theirs, Ivor Novello, in a show called *Gay's the Word* with Cicely Courtneidge. Vi and Gladys loved that show too but their favourite Ivor Novello musical was *The Dancing Years.* 'A lovely show – really gorgeous. Remember Roma Beaumont, the way she stood and sang that song, "Miss Primrose" – it was marvellous.'

Surely two of the most ardent theatregoers in London and always superbly dressed, the Bennett sisters are often the most elegant ladies in the audience. Dora Bryan calls them the 'Dolly Sisters' and well-groomed dollies they are too. They attend practically every first night and have been going to Drury Lane Theatre every Saturday night for over ten years, and they sometimes go twice a week. One week, they told me, they went to the Whitehall Theatre on the Monday, the Globe on the Wednesday, the Haymarket on the Thursday and Drury Lane on the Saturday.

Their life-long interest in the theatre they owe to their mother who, as a young woman, sang on the halls with Harry Champion. The Bennett sisters' mother, when she was only eighteen, also sang with The Foresters in the East End of London (where the sisters still live in the building where they were born). She gave up her stage career when she married and never sang again in public although her daughters never tired of hearing her voice and, so long ago that they can hardly remember it now, they decided that as soon as they were old enough they would try to get into the theatre. But they never attempted to work as performers and their only stage appearance has been in a Gilbert and Sullivan production at the local church hall.

The sisters first met Danny La Rue when they were working

for Vidrobes and they were asked to take some head-dresses to Churchills Club where he was then appearing. They met Danny, thought he was 'a cracker' and still feel the same way. Circumstances caused them to go back and forth several times and they began to get to know him. 'Off-stage he is very charming and handsome, with twinkling eyes and a saucy look – ever so nice,' they told me.

Danny had been booked at Churchills for two weeks. As he opened there was no applause whatever and that is the only time he has ever been greeted with silence. As he began to warm up, the *clientèle* loved his act. Danny sensed the initial hostility and said to himself, 'It's either you or them.' He closed to tremendous applause and stayed at Churchills for over three years. However, he has never forgotten how frightening that hostility was and he never completely relaxes on stage but is always nervous about the reactions of the audience.

It is nearly twenty years since Violet and Gladys Bennett first met Danny and nowadays it doesn't matter where he is or who he is with, as soon as he sees them he greets them with a wave and 'Hallo, Glad and Vi, come and give us a kiss!' He never ignores them. 'He's a gentleman in every way and yet he's a friend and a pal.'

A man who remembers his friends and especially those of the not-so-prosperous days, Danny often goes out of his way to greet people he has known a long time and the way in which he invariably salutes the Bennett sisters is perhaps a little thing to

him but means a great deal to them; often they are delighted to
see that he is wearing a lace or embroidered shirt-front that they
have made for him. They have also knitted four sweaters for him,
including an orange Aran, a great favourite.

At Danny's invitation the Bennett sisters went once to
Churchills Night Club and they have always remembered the visit
because they left somewhat hurriedly. During the course of one
act a lady artiste of somewhat ample proportions came among the
audience, selected a prosperous-looking patron and sat on his knee.
After a few familiarities she finished her act. Shortly afterwards the
man who had been favoured by her attentions suddenly started
screaming that his wallet containing over £50 had been stolen.
Gladys and Vi made a hurried exit; this was not at all their idea
of entertainment, but the cabaret was good and Danny was
wonderful, as always.

This incident reminds me of a story I heard recently;
something, I suppose that could only happen in 1974. A large
man was about to leave a London night club when he discovered
that his wallet was missing. A moment earlier a little man had
rushed past him. The big man immediately gave chase and caught
up with the little man as he was about to disappear into a taxi.
'Hey, you,' shouted the big man, grasping the little man's
shoulder with a huge hand, 'Where's the wallet?' Without a
murmur the wallet was handed over and when the big man
arrived home he found his wallet on his dressing-table!

Another incident the Bennett sisters cannot forget was a first night *Pyjama Tops* at the Whitehall Theatre (they have since seen it several times). They sat in the front row near the pool and when the show girls went into the pool the Bennett sisters were splashed, much to the amusement of the rest of the audience and Danny, four rows behind, stood up and called out, 'Hey, Glad and Vi, you got your bellies wet!'

After appearing at Churchill's and other West End clubs for ten years Danny opened his fantastically successful and expensive club in Hanover Square, a club that was to have over thirteen thousand paid up members and be packed every night. Probably the most successful night club London has ever seen, top show business personalities were always there, coach parties, Hollywood stars and even royalty. Princess Margaret and Lord Snowdon visited the club on the occasion of a celebration in the late 1960s (Lord Snowdon's secretary told me) and stayed late afterwards. Dame Margot Fonteyn and Rudolf Nureyev went three times to see themselves in the unforgettable impersonation by Danny and Ronnie Corbett. Lord Snowdon's mother, the Countess of Rosse, peered through the smoke on one occasion and asked: 'Who's that with the hooky nose?' It was Ringo Starr, visiting the club in happier times with his fellow Beatles. One of the few people who went there and left unimpressed, I am told, was Bette Davis.

There can be no doubt that the startling success of the club was entirely due to its owner and star performer, Danny. In the seven years that the club was open (it was finally closed when the lease expired and the demolition men moved in) Danny only missed one scheduled performance, when he had laryngitis.

Occasionally the Bennett sisters would go on to Danny's club after an evening at the theatre which they would leave about eleven o'clock. They might have a drink first, then get a taxi and stay at the club from about midnight until 3 am. Then a taxi home where they would arrive at maybe four or even five o'clock; have a rest for five or ten minutes and maybe a drink; wash and change, hang up their clothes, get ready for business and be back in their places at Nathans first thing that morning. Once they did this three nights in one week and still carried on with their exacting work. They hardly ever go to bed before two o'clock in the morning and are always up at six o'clock. They were born at the top of the building where they still live. At first their parents had two rooms and a little kitchen but as there were five girls eventually, the family moved into three rooms on the other side of the building. When they were about fourteen years old Vi and Gladys moved back to the other side of the house and they have now been in the same flat for fifty-five years. There were in all seven girls in the family – their father and mother never had any boys – and nearly all the girls grew up to be 'theatre mad'. They all learned to appreciate music and the theatre from their parents, both of whom had good singing voices. The two sisters still have a record that their mother made when she was seventy-eight, singing *Do a Good Turn When You Can.*

Alan Melville, during a broadcast of *These Are The Days* with Violet and Gladys Bennett, remarked: 'Danny La Rue has got a thing about you two girls, because he's told me so. I gather you make all Danny's fronts. Does this mean you make his false bra and his bosom?'

'Oh no,' the sisters protested. 'We make all the lace fronts and the *jabots*: the ornamental frills for evening wear.' Gladys makes all the long narrow ones by hand, she told me, and each one takes about seventy-five yards of lace.

It seems that on one occasion Danny was going somewhere special and looked for an embroidered shirt but couldn't get exactly what he wanted. He happened to tell Gladys who made him a front. He looked as though he was wearing a shirt and he was 'ever so pleased with it'. It is the only one of its kind.

The Bennett sisters look upon Danny as a 'real good chum and friend, one of the sweetest men.' They couldn't love him more if he was their own son and they are by no means alone. In the world of entertainment Danny is just as popular as he is with the public. Cyril Fletcher tells me he admires Danny enormously although he has some reservations about his playing Dame in pantomime. Not that this comment was meant to be in any way denigrating so far as his excellent performance as a comedian is concerned. 'He is,' said this individual and first-rate entertainer: 'a frightfully good performer and a great entertainer.'

Actor and comedian Richard Wattis says of Danny. 'As you may know, I worked with him in *Come Spy With Me* ... in a way his first move to the West End from pantomime, although his club was already flourishing. I can say honestly that he is an exceptionally kind and nice person, and quite an extraordinary worker. His artistry you will, of course, know all about, but what I want to say is that when we opened in Oxford for three weeks with *Come Spy With Me* and the curtain came down at 10.30 pm, make-up wise he finished as a man. It took two-and-a-half hours to be driven to London, make-up again as a woman, do his club show, drive back (arriving in Oxford about 5 am) sleep (?) and rehearse with us each day at 2.30 pm. That rigour also continued for one week at Brighton. His energy is quite phenomenal and his loyalty to his club (refusing to miss a show there even after a first night in the theatre) was a model of gratitude. Danny himself does not consider that he is a compulsive over-worker although he often did two shows a day and then a late night show at his club. 'The difference in the audiences keeps me fresh,' he said at the time. 'I don't get a chance to go stale.' Richard Wattis spoke for a great many people in show business and outside when he added: 'I join with the very, very many who say, and mean, "Good Luck always, Dan." '

Hard work is the lot of most people in show business but female impersonators in particular for they, both the successful and the less prominent, are professional performers and get paid to entertain. Often they work long hours for little money, in entertainment terms. They frequently give three shows a night, six nights a week and sometimes four shows on Saturdays.

Danny is fortunate in having been in show business a long time and in starting at the very bottom so that today he never needs a warm-up period; never needs to get into the mood. He steps straight on to the stage and it happens, every time.

He carries a lot of responsibility. He can't really have an understudy for instance, but he regards that as good for his health since he knows he can't miss a single show. He thinks fit and thinking fit keeps him fit.

He has never had a weight problem and remains steadfastly around the ten-stone-twelve-pound mark in spite of eating lashings of chips, baked potatoes, and other good food that he loves. He says, 'I suppose I've worked myself into a weight and it just sticks.'

Perhaps better than any other way an entertainer can be judged by the esteem – or otherwise – in which he is held by his fellow artistes. In the case of Danny La Rue the opinion is almost unanimous.

In 1973 I discussed Danny with the dedicated Midlands entertainer Larry Grayson in his dressing-room at the Lakeside Country Club, Frimley Green, before his cabaret act there, at a time when his second recorded series of *Shut that Door* was appearing on television.

Larry first met Danny La Rue in 1958; notoriously bad on dates, he remembers that one because he recalls that the play, *The Mousetrap* (which he could see advertised from his dressing-room window) was then in its seventh year. Larry had been playing in pantomime as Widow Twankey in *Alladin* at Manchester with Billy Danvers, then seventy years of age, as his son! Already Danny La Rue saw the makings of a big star in Larry Grayson and thereafter whenever he had the opportunity, during interviews on radio and television, Danny would mention Larry, 'an up and coming star' and say, 'There's a performer to watch; he's going to be a big hit.'

Twelve years later Larry and Danny met again at the Stork Room, London, and, although Larry hardly noticed it at the time, Danny asked him whether he had signed for *Birds of a Feather,* Paul Raymond's forthcoming drag show. Larry said he had, not realising that Danny was thinking of asking him to take his place at his London club while he was on holiday. During his annual holiday Danny had been in the habit of closing his Hanover Square Club but in Larry Grayson he had seen the one person whom he thought could take his place; a unique honour for Larry.

Later the Gallery First-Nighters held a party for Danny and, with Danny's approval, Larry Grayson was engaged to appear in cabaret. Now Danny knew he was right. 'You are going to be a big star,' he told Larry who replied, with characteristic honesty, 'Oh, I do hope so.'

That year, 1972, Larry was appearing in the summer season at Paignton and this time was able to accept when Danny asked him to take his place at the Club for a fortnight, while he was on holiday. Larry told me that he has never forgotten the courtesy and kindness that Danny showed him. He remembers that when he was shown into Danny's dressing-room, which was to be his for two weeks, Danny asked whether he would like anything moved or any alterations made, but it was all wonderful just as it was. And everyone at the Club was told personally by Danny: 'Mr Grayson is to be treated exactly as you would treat me. Anything he wants, he is to have.' And to Larry he added: 'You have only to ask.'

It was a real and wonderful opportunity for Larry and a generous gesture by Danny. Larry was fabulously successful. Danny's mother, who had not been well, turned up on the first night at 1.15 am saying she felt she had to see the boy who was taking her son's place. Afterwards she went round to his dressing-room, said she thought he had been wonderful and that she was delighted at his huge success.

At the end of the first week Larry asked for his personal bill which he knew must be well over thirty pounds. He was given a bill already signed, 'Paid, and thank you. Danny.' Next week, when Larry was asked what he wanted served in his dressing-room, he thought for a moment and then said, 'Oh, just a coffee, please.' 'Ah,' he was told. 'But this week you pay your own bill.' So he had a large gin and tonic. At the end of the week he again asked for his bill and exactly the same thing happened. His bill was paid, with thanks, by Danny who, knowing that Larry would not dream of taking advantage, had left instructions that he was to be told that he would pay his own bill the second week.

Understandably Larry Grayson has great admiration and affection for Danny La Rue and Danny, in his turn, is proud of the great faith he has always had in Larry. Once, when both Larry

and Danny were appearing at Manchester, Larry went to Danny's
show and watched it from a box. Danny spotted him and at the
end of the performance told the audience: 'We have a great
performer here this evening: Ladies and Gentlemen, Larry
Grayson,' and he pointed to the box. It was a rare tribute from
one artiste to another; as it was when Danny, working hard as
always at Manchester and very tired, nevertheless made a special
journey to be with Larry on *This is Your Life.*

It is good to know that such talented and in some ways very
similar entertainers have achieved great success and still show
kindness and thoughtfulness to other performers. The patter and
the acts of Larry Grayson and Danny La Rue are similar although,
as Larry says during the course of his cabaret act, he could never
wear the clothes that Danny wears, he has a thing about feathers
to start with; yet there is the same style, attention to timing,
professionalism and inoffensive suggestiveness. They are both
loved and admired by men and women in their audiences
(contrary to some drag artistes) and off-stage they are both
friendly, good-humoured, sincere and dedicated entertainers, and
they never talk smut. 'I did a drag act for years', Larry told me.
'But I never liked those lashes and wigs.' These days he
doesn't vary his forty-five minute cabaret act very much. He has
no need to. Television has made him famous and he has only to
say 'What a gay day' and everyone falls about. He says that he
and Danny have often talked of working together but they are too
much alike and yet perhaps one day, Larry will don drag while

Danny wears a suit. . . .

In March 1970, Wendy Craig, popular star of such series as *Not In Front of the Children,* was named Television Personality of the Year, the first woman ever to win the award. At the Savoy Hotel luncheon to mark the Variety Club's Showbiz Awards for 1969, Danny La Rue was named Showbusiness Personality of the Year and he received a silver heart for his conspicuous performance in the 1969 Royal Command Variety Show and his television and stage success. Danny was particularly pleased by this professional accolade from within the ranks of the entertainment industry. 'Any craftsman is especially pleased when he's given a tribute by his fellow artisan,' Danny told Peter Tipthorp in 1973. 'I love the theatre and for me that award was just marvellous.' Afterwards the two winners of the year's top awards from the Variety Club of Great Britain were photographed together. Wendy Craig has always adored Danny; 'a great guy.' She told me that she can't really say she knows him although she and her husband, journalist Jack Bentley, visited Danny's Club on one occasion and went backstage afterwards for a chat. She summed Danny up for me as 'a nice guy both in and out of drag.' The award came soon after Danny's very successful show had opened at the Palace Theatre. The presentation was made by impresario Bernard Delfont, a great friend of Danny's, who himself received a special award for his services to British entertainment.

John Mills, the distinguished actor and producer, was present with his wife Mary Hayley Bell on 9 June, 1970 at the Variety

Club's Seventeenth Annual Ladies' Luncheon, at the Dorchester
Hotel, and afterwards he and his wife posed for photographs with
Danny. John Mills was also with Danny at a get-together at the
Apollo Theatre on 21 December, 1971 when five famous actors
who had played the lead in *Charley's Aunt* (that dateless comedy
that has probably had more performances than any other stage
play) celebrated the anniversary of the first London production of
the Brandon Thomas play, on 21 December 1892. The five were
John Mills, Leslie Phillips, Philip Dale, Danny La Rue and, then
appearing in the latest production, Tom Courtenay. I asked John
Mills and his wife for their opinion of Danny. His reply was a
simple one; he said with great sincerity: 'We are great admirers of
Danny.'

What's a Girl Like You, London Weekend's television
documentary about drag entertainment carried many tributes to
Danny, from both audience and performers. But Danny hasn't
seen that programme and he says he has never seen a drag act in a
pub. 'I only have Sundays free,' he reminded an interviewer in
1972, 'and they're far too precious to me to have a busman's
holiday.' Anyway, he's not really interested. 'So many of the
performers are transvestites. They change after the show from
evening dress into skirt and blouse . . . they make me feel like a
lorry driver!'

Lord 'Ted' Willis invented the original story for Danny's film
Our Miss Fred and in reply to my approach to him, he said: 'I am
afraid that there is very little that I can give you which would

help towards your work on Danny La Rue. Although I invented
the original story for the film, my part in the production was a
very minimal one and I think I only saw Danny once during the
entire production. Apart from that I have only met him a couple
of times. This has not given me any real opportunity to get to
know him or to collect the kind of reminiscences that might be
useful to you. Of course, I do have a general impression. He is a
superb professional, a perfectionist who drives himself almost into
the ground in his ruthless pursuit of excellence. He is at the top
and remains at the top because he never allows himself to slip
from these self-imposed standards. He also has the other hallmark
of a truly great professional in that he is extremely generous
towards his fellow artists both on stage and off-stage.'

Gerry Slinger, managing director of Blighty's Club, Farnworth,
told me that he could not claim to be a friend of long standing
but he has been an avid fan of Danny's. I asked him for any
special memories and he said that what impressed him most about
Danny is the fact that Danny is a widely-acclaimed star who still
breaks records almost everywhere he goes; a star of great stature,
yet 'with a tremendous memory for the most trivial detail, like the
birthday of one of the theatre staff, and a million other things.'
'One of my most treasured memories' he added. 'Is being invited
out to dinner with Louis Benjamin of the London Palladium and a
host of really important people, and my wife was the only lady
present. The courtesy and consideration shown by Danny
generated to the other gentlemen present and made my wife, to

quote her own words, "feel like Elizabeth Taylor". He certainly is quite a guy and I could go on for ever . . . '

Part Three
The Early Years

CORK, ONE OF ITS SONS TOLD ME YEARS AGO, IS THE FINEST PLACE ON EARTH and with its white limestone buildings and terraced hills, has a continental air as attractive to visitors as it is haunting and unforgettable to those born within this fine city and seaport at the head of the beautiful river Lee. And among its sons is Daniel Patrick Carroll, a man destined to become the highest paid entertainer on the English stage, a man known today as Danny La Rue.

Danny was born in Cork on 26 July, 1927, the son of an interior decorator, a profession followed by Danny's brother Richard (Dick). Their mother, Mary Ann Carroll, was a nurse before she ran away from home when she was seventeen to marry a handsome sailor, Thomas Carroll. She had six children of whom Danny was the fifth. It seems that there have always been troubles in Ireland and that period was no exception. When the boy who was to lift the Carroll family from obscurity was only six, his father aged thirty-three, was killed. It is something that Danny has never forgotten and understandably it has coloured his whole outlook and not least his feelings on the continuing troubles in Ireland. In 1972 he said, when asked about his moral fervour: 'I loathe and detest what's going on in Ireland now. That is the real immorality.' 'The great tragedy of the world today,' he said on another occasion, 'is lack of trust. People just do not trust one another. So many people have to ask: "I wonder whether he means what he says?" Nothing is going to get better in the world until we start believing in each other again,' he told Peter

Tipthorp in 1973. 'That's the problem we all face in the future.'

Inevitably there were hard times, but times now recalled with affection by a devoted son; times when he and the other children were glad to have a meal that filled them; and times when Danny could eat almost anything, and he still enjoys eating and eating well.

The lessons of childhood are hard but lasting ones and often they are very beneficial. Today Danny doesn't smoke and he doesn't drink spirits but he loves champagne. Champagne is of course well known to be one of the few non-fattening drinks and for this reason it is popular with jockeys. Danny often takes it with orange juice, a drink known as 'Buck's Fizz'. He says he has seen what drink can do to so many people in his profession but he enjoys the odd glass of wine and he loves nougat. He has never forgotten his Roman Catholic upbringing. Today his faith means a lot to him and he needs the security of having a religion behind him. 'I wouldn't be without it,' he said in 1973. 'I pray, but mostly for other people. I find it more difficult to pray for myself.'

After she had been widowed, Mrs Carroll brought some of her family, including Danny, to England, and they settled in London but during the Second World War they moved to a Devon village near Exeter. At Kennford, Danny, his brother John and sister Nancy went to school and enjoyed their youth in the restful, pleasant and happy atmosphere of the Devonshire countryside. Those days provided Danny with vivid and happy memories in years to come: village life, amateur dramatics, Thursday dances, long cycle rides sometimes in rain, leafy Devon lanes.

Danny is still remembered in Kenn and the surrounding district
as one of the group of young village people who grew up there
in the postwar years. Mrs Honor Ratcliffe who still lives in the
village easily recalls Danny in his early days. In fact she went to
school with him at Kennford (the largest village in the parish of
Kenn) and today has many happy recollections of him and other
young people with whom they mixed.

At school, for instance, Mrs Ratcliffe (or rather Honor Preece as
she was then) remembers that Danny would spend much more
time drawing ladies' dresses than he did doing lessons; and
whenever the other boys used to rib him, Danny (even then never
at a loss for an apt rejoinder) would quickly take the wind out of
their sails with a few well-chosen words.

John R Waldron was troop leader of the Kenn St Andrews
Scout group, of which Danny was a member, during the early
part of the War. 'I knew Danny Carroll well,' said John Waldron
and he has a photograph of Danny as a boy scout peeling potatoes
for a stew to be cooked over an open fire at a weekend camp.

'Among our many activities we often had weekend camps at
Trehill, Kenn,' explained John Waldron. 'Danny lived with his
family in a cottage on Trehill estate, at the time, so we virtually
camped on his own doorstep.

'He was very keen on scouting and quickly learnt such things
as first aid, cookery and the morse code. He was also a keen
swimmer and frequented the local outdoor swimming-pool at

Friars.

'I never knew Danny to be anything but immaculate in his appearance; he was always "one of the gang" but he was invariably well-mannered and unassuming.'

Until my research in the Exeter district revealed in the local newspapers the fact that Danny La Rue was Daniel Carroll, John Waldron was one of the people who knew Danny in his youth but had no idea that he was in fact the famous Danny La Rue.

Jim Ratcliffe (Honor's husband) taught Danny to ride a bicycle and somehow or other every time Danny fell off, he landed in a bed of stinging nettles! But he shrugged off the stings and the discomfort and persevered until he could ride. 'He was like that,' said Mrs Ratcliffe. 'He just would not give up.'

There was something of a Kennford 'young set' in the village in those days and Danny was a popular member. Already he was a good dancer. 'A lovely dancer, really,' recalled Mrs Ratcliffe who often partnered him in his teenage dancing years. 'Not that he was a special friend or anything for we all used to go around together.'

After leaving school Danny set about earning some money to help with the family income and in the years immediately following, he washed dishes, dressed windows, did night-work at an ice-cream factory and helped behind the scenes at theatres.

Mrs Peggy Reeves, who now lives at Whipton near Exeter, worked with Danny when he began work as a shop assistant and window dresser at Huttons, an outfitting store that stood at the lower corner of Queen Street, Exeter towards the end of the War.

She and her sister, surnamed Mitchell in those days, both worked at Huttons and until August 1973 Mrs Reeves had no idea that the handsome young man she used to work with was Danny La Rue.

'Our staff at Huttons was a small but happy one,' she told me. 'There were Mr and Mrs Payne, the manager and manageress; the cashier Agnes Goldsworthy (later Mrs Lukan); a Miss Taliday, first sales assistant; my sister Una Mitchell (now deceased), Danny and myself. In addition there were three workroom ladies; two sisters, the Misses Edwards and Miss O'Reilly.

'Danny was not always referred to as Danny by my sister and me; we called him Jammy for the simple reason that he would often share our lunches, consisting mostly of doughnuts and chocolate biscuits, and if we cut a doughnut in half, you could be sure that Danny would get the half with the jam! I said to him one day, "Danny, you've got the jam again, you should be called Jammy, not Danny!" He thought it quite a joke at the time.

'Some lunch-times Danny would accompany Una and me when we went window-shopping. He always liked company I remember, but most of all I remember his good looks, sleek dark hair, flashing eyes and the most infectious giggle. I don't believe that I ever heard him give a good hearty laugh; but once he started giggling his shoulders would shake and he'd have us all going. Yes, even in those far off days he had the ability to make others laugh ... although I must not mislead you. It wasn't always roses

all the way with us; in fact I rather think that if Danny
remembers me at all, it will be on account of our differences of
opinion.'

Peggy Reeves remembers that Danny was somewhat
over-anxious to help on occasions, to the extent that at times he
seemed to be under everyone's feet and at least twice she recalls
that she and Danny had words; and at such times 'Danny could
be quite fiery.' 'Danny was a very determined person, with a mind
of his own, and a definite view-point from which no one could
deter him. Yet, in spite of everything they really were happy days
... No hard feelings Danny over our few battles of words,' says
Peggy Reeves. 'I feel proud to have known you.'

At this time everyone felt that Danny was attracted to Peggy's
sister, Una. 'My sister could not move for him,' Mrs Reeves
recalls. 'He was her shadow. In fact we used to tease him and tell
him he had a crush on her, and he never denied it.'

Mrs Agnes Lukan (formerly Goldsworthy) also recalled for me
those early days at Huttons with Danny (when she was a young
bride) and in fact she distinctly remembers Danny's first day at
work when he was brought round by the manager and introduced
as a new assistant.

'Mr and Mrs Payne managed the shop and they lived at
Kennford. At the time I understood that Danny and his family
had been evacuated from London. Mr and Mrs Payne brought
Danny along to work in the shop to learn window dressing.'

Looking back Agnes Lukan says 'Danny was a very pleasant and good-looking boy,' and she and Danny always got along famously and they had some wonderful times together. She recalls that Danny, even then, was fond of dressing-up and sometimes, when he was supposed to be dressing the shop window, he would pick up a length of veiling and some artificial flowers, give himself a buttonhole and her a 'bouquet'; and together they would parade round the department dressed as bride and bridegroom, until people started taking too much notice!

'After we had got to know him we had such fun. There was never a dull moment. I was employed as cashier-bookkeeper in the office downstairs with the millinery department. Dan would say, "Let's have a bit of fun", and we would both put on the funniest hats we could find, he would get some flowers from the window and we would walk round the corner of Queen Street, looking in the windows! I always remember how people stopped to look at us and then we would laugh so much that we just had to go back into the shop.

'Once I dressed as a bride with Dan as the bridegroom and we had another young girl as bridesmaid; this was quite fantastic. Naturally we did all this when there was no one around.

'At this time we had to have clothing coupons for everything and one morning Dan came in looking very sad and he said: "Do you think you could let me have some coupons for my sister?" He told me his sister had lost her husband. I think he was killed in the War. One just couldn't refuse him – he had such a charming way. I said, "Well, I'll see what I can do, Dan." After that of course Dan was always coming back for more. Very often he would bring me flowers from Kennford and he was so pleased to give them to me.' Danny, even then, liked to be immaculate in his appearance; he so enjoyed being well-dressed that Agnes Lukan admits she 'fiddled' a few coupons for him too.

'He was a very willing boy and if anyone wanted anything done, he never refused. I wonder if he remembers how he would always smooth the top of my head when he was talking to me?

'Dan was a very good-mannered and lovable boy. He was always telling us about his family; he thought such a lot of them. I met his mother on several occasions. Dan always kept himself very nice, and his hair was always well groomed.

'One day, when Dan and I had dressed up and the rest of the staff were looking over the banisters, watching us, the millinery buyer came in unexpectedly from lunch. She was furious, as we had taken her hats from the drawers. She called us a couple of clowns and said we had no business working in a shop!'

But still, whenever he had the opportunity, at lunch or tea breaks for example, Danny would encourage Agnes to dress up in hats and costumes and they would sometimes do a little act together. Mrs Lukan has always known that Danny La Rue is the friend with whom she enjoyed so many hours and whenever she has seen him on television she remembers the fun they had and she says she would love to meet him again, just 'for old times' sake.'

Agnes and her husband, a Czechoslovakian who also knew

Danny quite well, lost touch with Danny when he was promoted to a London branch of the store and only heard of him again when he began to achieve fame as 'king of drag'. Not that his success came as any surprise to Mrs Lukan. 'He was always so ready for fun, and he was so very artistic. He had lovely hands, with long, slender fingers. . .'

Danny's sister, Nancy, married a Kennford boy, Percy Christopher, who was tragically killed in the War. After his death she moved to London.

Danny's mother now lives in Hampstead and, says Danny: 'I'm sure she doesn't see the feathers and the furs. She just sees me.' He is grateful for the confidence and understanding that he has always received from his family. When he told them about his success as a drag artiste, they didn't bat an eyelid but then, he says, 'Every Irishman is an actor at heart and every Carroll believes in freedom.' He feels that his family have helped him keep his feet on the ground in the heady world of show business, though they do regard him as comparable to the office boy who became managing director. Yet Danny's soft Irish brogue still comes through when he is relaxed, especially in the pronunciation of such words as 'anyway'. He can, of course, speak with a broad Irish accent and will do so at the least provocation.

In 1944, when he was seventeen, Danny joined the Royal Navy and served for three years. While in the Navy he volunteered to join the ship's concert party, having discovered that the players were excused normal duties. He was posted to Singapore and lived a blissful year there. He enjoyed the concert parties, playing such parts as Tondelayo (the West African bombshell who created havoc among the white men on the station), in Leon Gordon's *White Cargo*. This first part was – prophetically – a native girl dressed in a 'sarong' (really a sheet) and since his lines were mundane in the extreme, being limited in that production to such expressions as 'Me go' and 'Me come back', Danny concentrated on make-up and 'costume' and was rewarded with ovations far in excess of those warranted by the part he played. All he can clearly remember now of that first part was how cold it was! Actually this was not his début as a female for he had, as a boy, appeared as Juliet in a school production of *Romeo and Juliet*, performed in a Devon village hall. Although he did not know it at the time he had already struck oil in much the same way as horror actor Boris Karloff did when he played the Demon King at the age of nine. When Danny was that age he had had a part in a production of *Cinderella*.

Childhood can be full of mimicry and already, unconsciously, Danny had discovered his *forte* in imitating female adults; a gift that was to stand him in good stead in the years to come.

He also discovered that not only did he enjoy playing female parts but that he was extremely good at it and this encouraged him to repeat the activity whenever the opportunity occurred. And so, deep in the unconscious of the young boy was sown the seed that was to germinate and blossom in adulthood to produce an unparalleled performer who would win, as no man in woman's

clothes had ever done before, acceptance from the man in the
street and approval from such dramatic critics as Ivor Novello and
Clive Barnes. Danny La Rue was the first man to make a fortune
out of dressing up as a woman; to appear before the Queen of
England dressed as a glamorous woman and to make female
impersonation really respectable.

During his time with the Royal Navy Danny, as we have seen,
was in the Far East and years later was to comment that he had
seen much of the world and enough to make him an extremely
tolerant human being.

As is known, the East has always been notorious for its
preoccupation with sex in all its forms. Japan has openly boasted
that prostitution was at one time its fourth largest industry.
Luridly pornographic paintings, prints, carvings and other erotica
from Japan are to be found in museums and private collections
throughout the world, and Japan has always been the principal
centre for the manufacture of erotic devices, implements and
apparatus. Homosexual and lesbian brothels have flourished there
for centuries and Tokyo lesbian cabarets abound, with practically
nude young women walking from table to table selling dildoes
and other erotic objects.

In China, too, homosexuality and diverse sexual activities have
been practised for at least a thousand years. Animals that have
been trained to copulate or have other sexual relations with
humans have long been an established and famous 'attraction' in
the East and in China in particular where dogs and small horses

have been used in erotic exhibitions with prostitutes.

Today the sirens of Singapore are different again, for the nubile young 'kytais' of Bugis Street and elsewhere, in fetching silk miniskirts, with beautiful hair, magnificent make-up and delightful breasts (made in Hong Kong of glycerine) are all boys. Yet it must be said that for all his extensive travels there is no evidence whatsoever that Danny La Rue ever encountered any of these activities or 'aids'.

The kytais must be drag at its ultimate and they are a far cry from Danny La Rue's funny, sophisticated performances that are the result of years of hard work, expensive costumes, beautiful wigs, and elaborate make-up. Danny himself once described his career as 'No stroke of luck but a natural progression, deliberately planned over the years.'

Back in England – and out of the Navy – at twenty years of age, Danny worked for a time with the old Theatre Royal repertory company in Exeter, as a sort of assistant stage manager. His duties included lots of scenery shifting and he was paid a wage of £5 a week. Still Danny was unsure of his potential at this time and the prospects did not look very good. In fact the theatre closed a few years later and was ultimately demolished. The *clientèle* for repertory in Exeter is now catered for at the Northcott Theatre.

Danny decided to try his hand again at fashion design and display and worked as a window dresser at Exeter and later in London; but as time passed he found the call of the stage

Above: A sketch (Danny in centre) from *Call It a Day* by Dodie Smith.

Below: Danny, extreme right, in the YWCA revue *Call It a Day.*

Left: A young Daniel Carroll (later Danny La Rue) in the YWCA production of *April Folly.*

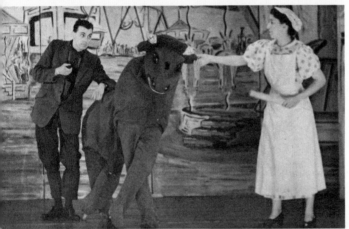

Left: Daniel Carroll (Danny La Rue) in the YWCA production of *April Folly.*

Below: The full cast of *April Folly* with Danny on the extreme right.

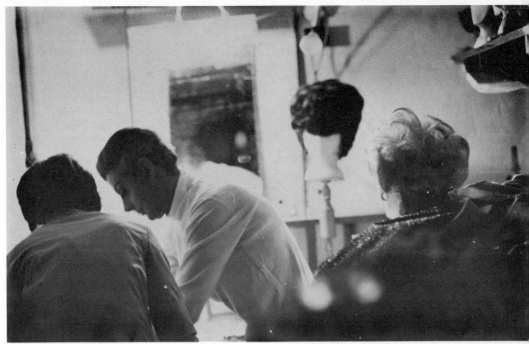

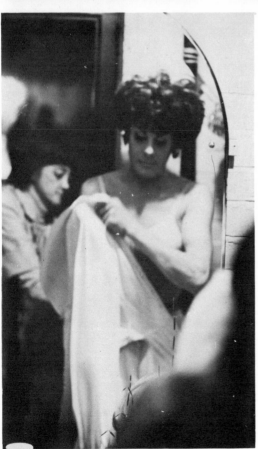

Rare photographs of Danny La Rue
backstage as the transformation takes place,
1966.

Danny with Mary Talbot's portrait at the Trafford Galleries, London. April 1967.

becoming stronger instead of weaker and he determined to get
into the theatre and work there full-time. He joined a dramatic
society and found himself a member of the Young Women's
Christian Association which in those days could include members
of the Young Men's Christian Association.

Miss J M Nelson, the Personal Assistant to the National
General Secretary of the YWCA, recalls that members of the
Carroll family came to the Central Club in Great Russell Street,
Bloomsbury, in the 1940s, so Danny knew the building as a
boy. The gymnasium of the club was turned into a public air raid
shelter and people used to come and sleep there during the
bombing raids. She remembers that the Carrolls lived in or near
Earnshaw Street, off New Oxford Street, at the time and Mrs
Carroll would come to the shelter with Danny and Nancy; and
later with another son.

Mrs Pauline Simond (formerly Pauline Stewart), who now lives
in Richmond, Surrey, was Drama Adviser to the YWCA Central
Club during the war years. Her duties included organising and
running activities for YWCA members. These included Acting
and Movement classes, production of Nativity plays, pantomimes,
straight plays and musicals, in addition to supervising play-reading
groups, theatre party outings and recitals of poetry and music. She
remembers that young Danny Carroll joined in some of these
'mixed' activities because one of the first things she did on taking
up her appointment was to break down as fast as she could the
existing tradition of all-female activities, which were, as she puts

it, death and destruction to drama!

Her policy in this respect was so successful that within two or three years the YWCA had a flourishing drama department consisting of some sixty enthusiastic members, including a number of young men who joined either from the YMCA establishment just across the road (which appeared to run little lively drama at that time) or who were introduced by women club members from among their own friends.

Danny Carroll joined *via* the London Central YMCA and immediately became absorbed into the warm and friendly informality of whatever was going on. He was described to me, even at this early period of his life, as 'outgoing, amusing, very kind, always slightly outrageous but never in any way insolent or insensitive.' Inevitably, as thousands were to do in later years, the girls, the older members and the club leaders, adored him, for already he had great charm, abundant humour and generosity in his dealings with people.

In particular Mrs Simond remembers him in a Dodie Smith play entitled *Call It a Day,* which deals in a light-hearted manner with the effects of the first day of spring on the members of a family. Danny played the eighteen-year-old son of the household who is saved from an unsuitable relationship with the slick, money-spending, no-good Alec, with his fast cars and cheap values, by falling in love with the girl next door! Mrs Simond distinctly recalls sometimes having to control Danny's humorous exuberances in performance which threatened to 'burst out' of the style of the play as a whole, but she never had to ask him to 'project more'! 'Already he had that thousand-watt brilliance as a performer that comes zinging over in everything he does now,' she said.

She recalled for me an incident she has never forgotten in connexion with this particular production, produced in the days of severe clothes rationing. Curtains were needed for the two french windows on the set, but no one had any clothing coupons to spare with which to buy material. Danny was at that time working as a window dresser and shop assistant for a firm with a name like Charco's and he managed to borrow two lengths of blue Moygashel linen material which were duly draped to create effective curtains and pelmets.

'Alas,' Mrs Simond continued, 'before they could be returned to Danny's boss, they were stripped off the set one night and pinched, presumably by someone who was tempted by their obvious possibilities as summer dress material at that time of severe rationing! In fear and trembling I wrote an abject letter to Danny's boss apologising and explaining what had happened and I can still remember his reply: "The loss of the material, though regrettable, does not matter very much." ' Mrs Simond tells me that she thought at the time, and still thinks, that it must have been something to do with Danny's persuasive charm that his boss was not irate at the loss of irreplaceable window dressing.

Danny took part in a few other shows that were put on by the YWCA, revues like *April Folly* and *The Black and White* and he featured in some pantomimes there too. Mrs Simond, who went on to produce plays at the New College of Speech and Drama (of which she was a co-founder and is currently Director of Drama) and opera at the Royal Academy of Music, has produced many, many shows but she still remembers, vividly and with affection, the attractive young man who was to become Danny La Rue.

Mrs Esmé Cooper of Dulwich was a member of the YWCA Central Club Drama Group in those days and she can only distinctly recall Danny appearing in the two shows, *April Folly* and *Call It a Day.* The former was a 'New Spring Revue', a number of incidents strung together by a theme that ran throughout the show. This was in fact Pauline Stuart's first attempt at scriptwriting and Danny was the 'back end of a cow', in the 'Rustic Bliss' item. The front of the cow was Sheila Collins. It 'caused quite a stir' at the YWCA that the cow's costume was shared by two people of the opposite sex and it was thought by many to be representative of the 'downfall of the young generation!' Danny also played the part of a puppet in the sketch 'Hi Diddle De Dee'.

The first full-length play put on by the YWCA Central Club was *Call It a Day,* a comedy in three acts, produced on three consecutive evenings for Club members and their friends, at the Queen Mary Hall, with the proceeds going towards new lighting equipment. Mrs Cooper mentions that Danny, at that time, found it difficult to relax when on stage.

The coffee bar situated below the flat where Danny lived with his family, at Cambridge Circus, was the favourite club rendezvous, and Mrs Cooper recalls that 'he was well liked by the girls and they nearly all wanted to mother him.' Everyone was very concerned when he left and went into the 'legitimate' theatre and it was a great surprise to some of the old members of the society to hear that he had made such a success of his career.

By now Danny was convinced beyond any shadow of a doubt that acting was what he really wanted. Somehow he must get into the theatre full time. He had been bitten by the theatrical bug, an affliction for which there is no known cure.

Learning of a possible opening he turned up one day at an audition for a chorus boy and, somewhat to his surprise, got the job and went on tour for a year with an all-male show which he recalls as *Forces Showboat,* followed by others with less prim titles such as *Soldiers in Skirts.* Looking back on this period of his life Danny says that at the time he hated it. 'The others were so serious and they loved dressing-up whereas I didn't seem to be able to do anything right. Do you know that the most difficult thing to do on the stage is to stand still? That sort of thing has to be learned.' 'I have done things on stage that I would be horrified to do now, but that was because I didn't know any better,' he told an interviewer in 1972. It was in fact a depressing time for him. He had been on the point of getting married but things had not worked out and he found stage work gave him renewed confidence in himself and helped enormously.

For something like eight years he toured Britain with various shows. At one period he was in variety with Harry Secombe for fourteen months. That particular show finally petered out in Bristol just before Christmas, having taken practically no money the previous week. This meant that the artistes received little or no pay, and some of them, including Danny, were unable to find even the fare home for the holiday. Harry Secombe generously paid the fares; it was the week that his daughter Jenny was born.

Still Danny stuck to stage work and did everything there was to be done: work behind the scenes, chorus boy, dancer, drag, anything; he didn't earn much money but he gained invaluable experience. During those long years of apprenticeship he never earned more than seven pounds a week and nearly starved on occasion but knew that he was learning the craft of what he was determined to do. Just once, when things really got on top of him and he felt that he was getting nowhere, he gave up and went back to work in a fashion shop or, as he puts it, to 'the rag trade'. But he was totally miserable there and as soon as another opportunity came along, back he went to stage work.

Gradually he thought he was getting used to the routine. Practice had made him an excellent dancer and he appeared in the chorus of some of the leading all-male shows that originated in Army Camp entertainment where no girls were available. Many holidaymakers saw Danny without knowing it in shows with titles like *Forces in Petticoats* at the then Margate Theatre, but entertaining as those shows were Danny began to see that he was unlikely to achieve any real and lasting success in them so eventually he left, but not until he had toured most of Britain and played in practically every music hall in the country. These frantic revues, in his opinion, with their uneasy titles, are completely contrary in tone and outlook to Danny's later clean-cut approach to drag and drag entertainment.

Nevertheless all-male revues were tremendously popular in the years immediately following the Second World War, as was the celebrated *Splinters,* in several editions, after the First World War when this 'revusical vaudeville' played to capacity houses at the old Queen's Theatre in Shaftesbury Avenue and many provincial theatres for nearly twenty years. In the late 1940s and well into the 1950s such shows as *Soldiers in Skirts, Forces in Petticoats, Showboat Express, Forces Showboat* and *Misleading Ladies* (in which Danny had his first speaking part) filled a need and gave audiences a chance to laugh, for a change, at and with the men who personified the soldiers, sailors and airmen to whom the relaxing theatregoers felt they owed so much.

'I can't really see the point,' Danny said, twenty years later. 'I could see the point of dressing-up as a bird to get laughs, but not to be serious.' 'A lot of the boys liked dressing-up as women and would have dressed up for nothing,' he told Russell Miller of *Daily Mirror Magazine* in May 1970. 'Many of them got to the point where they could have been girls; there was no reference to their being anything else until the very end of the show when they took their wigs off. I always thought it was completely and utterly revolting to see a man's head in a woman's make-up.'

But the lure of the stage still held him. Ted Gatty, the comedian, compère and producer, was a friend of Danny's in those days and helped him on the road to fame, not least by giving Danny the name by which he has been known ever since.

Ted first saw Danny when he was in the chorus of some of the drag shows, as a 'parade'. When the drag shows finished Danny worked as a male model and on window display for the fashion department of an Oxford Street store and there Ted met him again. 'I was then working in cabaret at Churchills Club in Cecil Landeau's Floor Show and I had just taken the Irving Theatre in Leicester Square with the intention of presenting and appearing in Late Night Revue.

'I asked Danny whether he would be interested in coming in with us on a "commonwealth" basis as there would be no salaries, the theatre only having a seating capacity of seventy-five! Danny was interested all right but he was not all that keen. However when he learned that it was only for two weeks, he said: "All right, but you can't use my name. The store wouldn't like it."

'I said, "leave it to me", and when he came to rehearse at the theatre I had already had some posters produced and they were on display outside with the artistes' names. Danny wanted to know which one was him and I said : "That's you, Danny La Rue!" ' It has been suggested that when he was all dressed up in drag Danny looked as long as a street and that is how the 'La Rue' came into being! Be that as it may, Danny duly appeared for the first time under his new name in the Ted Gatty revue, *Men Only,* and, feeling that perhaps the name would be a lucky one for him, he continued to use it thereafter. How right he was.

Other drag artistes have acquired their stage names just as lightly. Bristol-born Jim Wyatt was still using his real name when he was about to appear in drag for the first time at the Escort Club. The manager hurriedly suggested 'Miss Smith' as an obvious pseudonym but Jim didn't like that so 'Mister Smith' was suggested. Time for his entry on stage had by now arrived and he stepped forward, introduced as 'Mister Smith'. He has retained that name and built for himself a considerable following as a comedian in tasteful make-up and beautiful clothes for, like Danny, he can invest female impersonation with something far in excess of the immediate visual joke. Jim Wyatt used to remove his wig at the end of his act but, like Danny and some other drag performers, he no longer feels that this somewhat grotesque sight is necessary, especially as he removes his bra at the end of his striptease act!

'Danny's appearance in *Men Only* was the beginning of a very long association,' continued Ted Gatty. 'Danny soon forgot the window dressing bit. Cecil Landeau saw him in the Irving show and booked him with me at Churchills Club, and we played for several years at Winstons, the Bagatelle, The 21 Room and elsewhere; and of this period, as you may guess, we have many strange memories and happenings of the night club scene!' Ted Gatty went on to mention that he had only recently concluded a 'fantastic run at the Palace Theatre, Manchester, with Danny as

"Queen of Hearts" and myself as the Queen Mother and the sheer magic of Danny's rapport with the audience is like the late Max Miller, "the pure gold of music hall" '.

In the world of British drag, Rex Jameson stands alone. His unique character, 'Mrs Shufflewick', is a drab and middle-aged woman, clutching her handbag and maintaining a constant diatribe, visually a long way from Danny's immaculate characters. Yet many people consider that this true artiste, impressive and polished, has an almost unbelievable sense of timing that leaves even the remarkable Danny La Rue far behind. Jameson is in fact a comedian in women's clothing; a pub entertainer whose jokes have become more *risqué* as the sexual climate has become more permissive.

Rex Jameson was once a member of Ralph Reader's *Gang Show,* an unlikely but valuable starting place for impersonators. Ralph Reader appeared in three Royal Command Performances and presented no less than a hundred and twenty shows at the Royal Albert Hall. He produced annually his famous *Gang Shows* from 1937 onwards and some of the boys and young men taking part in these all-male shows discovered that they had a remarkable flair for female impersonation, most outstanding among these artistes (apart from Rex Jameson) was Billy Wells who began his stage career in 1928 but turned to drag while he was in the Royal Air Force during the War, when he took part in productions of the *Gang Show.* He was also in *Forces Showboat* with Danny.

Ralph Reader tells me that several later drag artistes took part in his first *Gang Show* and he remarked on the fact that wartime seems (perhaps understandably) to produce some of the best drag shows: *Splinters* and a Canadian Show immediately came to his mind, both very popular after the First World War; and during and after the Second World War the RAF *Gang Show* was very successful, especially after the great tour Ralph Reader made with the show for Tom Arnold and the eventual seven months in the West End at the Stoll Theatre. 'In "civvy street",' he told me, 'the show ran for well over two years.'

I asked Ralph about his personal views on drag for, to a certain extent, he is responsible for the popularity of the drag shows that are today part of British entertainment. He replied: 'My own view of drag is that it is not, I'm afraid, something I am crazy about. Brought to the fine art of Danny La Rue, well, that's part and parcel of show business. Rex Jameson, on the other hand, is equally good. I mean that. In his way he is a pocket edition of a Marie Lloyd and he explodes talent in a saucy yet pathetic way. If circumstances had been different he would have been as big a star (in an entirely different way) as Danny.'

Rex Jameson – or rather Mrs Shufflewick – appeared on and off at the one and only Windmill Theatre for two years; then in its heyday as a theatre of variety. He often met a young man called Danny Carroll who was just beginning a new life at the little Irving Theatre as Danny La Rue. The two artistes used to relax over a Guinness in Leicester Square. Danny, it seems, has graduated to champagne but 'Shuff' still enjoys a Guinness.

Shuff's costumes are of course in striking contrast to the incredibly beautiful and specially-designed outfits that are worn by Danny. Rex told me that he originally dressed his 'Mrs Shufflewick' as he thought charwomen dressed, shabby and slovenly, a jumper with holes in it and a tatty feather boa. Then one evening Betty Driver (later to appear behind the bar in *Coronation Street*) suggested to him that it could add a dimension to his act if his character appeared in good clothes. Rex tried it, found it successful and has so dressed ever since. Much of his original and unique wardrobe has in fact been picked up at market stalls and in Oxfam shops.

At first Danny didn't tell his mother that he was doing drag, Victor Spinetti told me, and he has often wondered what she would have thought if she had opened the suitcase Danny kept under his bed and found all the ladies' clothes inside!

The opportunity for Danny to work in cabaret, as a female impersonator, at Churchills Club in Bond Street, in London's Mayfair, and other work that followed gave him an invaluable ringside view of all the best variety and show stars of the day at work. He always watched and listened to the stars. 'That's how I learned', he says. He never had any drama training but with the help and encouragement of people like Ted Gatty and Rex Jameson and the wonderful opportunity to work at Churchills, at last Danny had arrived.

Part Four
The Long Climb
to the Top

IT WAS IN 1952 THAT DANNY WENT TO CHURCHILLS IN BOND STREET, (AND occupied a dressing-room about the size of a closet) and there he specialised in his new brand of female impersonation and became, almost overnight, a star. He saw a new approach to the Douglas Byng tradition of impersonation and developed his act, facing, apart from the usual club members, the occasional tough, rough, drunk and noisy interruption with an outward calm and assurance that belied the inner anxiety and was quite astonishing in one so young: he was still under twenty-five.

On the first night there was no reaction at all from the audience and Danny came off and thought to himself, 'Well, that's it, I've had it.' And then someone went up to him and said his act was wonderful, fantastic, they'd never known the diners *listen* before, they were usually too busy chatting up the birds. It was all the encouragement he needed.

Danny's act improved and he began to be well-received. He became popular and respected for his up-to-the-minute patter, his already immaculate attire and his almost uncanny sense of timing, especially when telling his blue jokes. At last he felt able to project himself as he had always wanted to be seen by his audience: fast and funny, sophisticated and vulgar. These were the years of rehearsal for his own club, and slowly but surely he built up his stock of unique and usually aggressive characters: Lady Cynthia Grope (that mainstay of the Conservative Party), a larger-than-life teenage rocker, a fanciful Japanese geisha girl, a bold and hard stripper, and other dubious ladies; and his staggering collection of blue jokes.

There was rarely a hint of any feminine charm or delicacy in his characterisations; they were the assertive, high-powered, career women of the day. But he created a remarkable illusion of glamour which the *clientèle* of Churchills loved and he stayed there for three years. Among the many incidents at Churchills that revealed Danny's art of repartee and incidentally provided him with lines that he used for years afterwards was the occasion on which one of the club hostesses was trying to entice a boy friend who was paying more attention to Danny than he was to her. This was too much and in front of everyone she suddenly pulled down her shoulder straps and bared her breasts for his inspection, adding, 'Look, these are real.' Like lightning Danny called out: 'Yes, darling they are, but I can hang mine up when it's hot!'

In 1955 Danny moved to Winston's Club, just across the road, and he appeared there for nearly seven years, presenting night after night with growing professionalism the brassy ladies in their lacquered pagoda wigs, extravagant baroque gowns and emphatic *décolletage*.

It was while he was there that Danny met Ronnie Corbett with whom he was to appear in some memorable and hilarious acts. Ronnie Corbett, once described as the only professional funny man who is also a happy man, was born in Edinburgh where he was educated and worked for two years as a civil servant before joining the Royal Air Force in 1949 for his national service. There he became Personnel Selection Officer and Camp Entertainments

Officer although his only experience of entertaining had been a church Youth Club pantomime in which he had played a wicked aunt in *Babes in the Wood,* drag already!

After his national service he decided to see whether he could make entertainment his career and managed to get a few engagements at pubs, clubs and in revues. He was introduced to Winstons Club by Digby Wolfe and there Danny invited him to stay and work with him. Afterwards he went to Danny's club and acted as 'feed man' to Danny in many sketches; Ronnie taking such parts as Napolean, Caesar and Toulouse-Lautrec in satires on famous couples in history.

While working with Danny, Ronnie Corbett was seen several times by David Frost and while Ronnie was in the ill-fated *Twang,* David Frost invited him to tea at the Ritz and there offered him a part in his then forthcoming television show, *The Frost Report.* So successful was this that Ronnie went on to appear in two editions of that series and also did a half-hour show with David Frost. This all helped tremendously and work followed in pantomime, summer shows and cabaret, where he occasionally appears with his wife whom he met at Winstons. Like many successful club entertainers today Ronnie Corbett is deeply grateful to Danny La Rue for help and encouragement in the early days of his professional career.

Another of Danny's partners at Winston's was Maggie Fitzgibbon and in September 1973 I asked her for her impressions of Danny and any particular memories and anecdotes, following her many appearances with him before she became a successful straight actress. But she told me that she is not an 'anecdotal actress, unfortunately', but she continued: 'More to the point is the fact that I should like to say that I enjoyed working with Danny, and I do mean working with, as he and I did, over a period of working at Winstons night club for nine months, a number of stand-up routines and songs together.

'The thing that I remember so vividly at that time was the fact that the climate for someone working in "drag" was not as it is now and Danny had not reached the zenith of his popularity, which in other words meant that on occasions he was doing battle with somewhat unsympathetic audiences, and in all that time he remained the victor, by sheer dint of his hard-core professionalism and humour. I don't use the word "professionalism" with abandon! It was, and is, Danny's prime attribute that he cares meticulously about the way he presents himself. He knows what people want and expect of him, and he gives it. That's a pro!

'I wish I could think of amusing incidents; I can't, but I know there will be others able to provide these aspects. Thank you for being interested in what I might have to say.'

I am grateful to Maggie Fitzgibbon for taking time off while rehearsing a new play to write to me about Danny and I am particularly glad to have her comments for there are many people who recall with pleasure her appearances with Danny as some of the best sketches he has appeared in, thanks in no small measure to the artistry and talent of Maggie Fitzgibbon, a real 'pro' herself.

Talented actor Victor Spinetti told me that he has always admired Danny for his brilliant repartee. He remembers one occasion at Winstons when some of the customers threw ice cubes at Danny during his impression of Mae West. Quick as a flash Danny turned on the offending party and called out: 'Hey! Who do you think I am, Sonja Henie?'

At Winstons Club, where Danny put on a completely new show every three months, he took a great deal of trouble to ensure that the show was first-class in every respect and after appearing he would mingle with the audience, often until five o'clock in the morning.

During one of his many chats with Danny, Victor recalls that there was some discussion about Danny altering his act but he said, no, he would stick to what he knew, and become a national star. No one can dispute that he made the right decision. Victor has always remembered that Danny said on another occasion, when talking about the entertainment industry: 'There's plenty of room at the top but no room at the bottom.'

Victor told me too the inside story of Danny's departure from Winstons which he had made into a successful club with his tremendous personality and stunning impersonations. After seven years there Danny felt that he was entitled to more than an artiste's fee and he approached the then owner with the suggestion that he should become a partner. The owner turned down the idea in no uncertain manner and Danny found himself out of a job. He decided to take the risk and open his own club, in partnership with a friend. They were fortunate in finding premises in Hanover Square and the club became one of if not the most successful that London has ever seen.

The tremendous success of the club was of course due to a very large extent to Danny himself but, especially in the early days, Victor Spinetti helped enormously by telling people about the club and it was through him that such people as Lord Snowden and Princess Margaret, Barbara Windsor, and the Beatles all went to the club in the first place; tremendously increasing the prestige and popularising the club as *the* London night club of its time.

Victor, of course, knew the Beatles well and he has appeared in all their films; in fact it was while making a film with them that he took them to Danny's club. So regularly did Victor take guests to the club – just about everyone he knew, he told them all 'you must go to Danny's' – that he had a permanently reserved table, known as 'Victor's table'.

Danny has always kept his personal self and the act of female impersonation in two distinct compartments of his life. In the early days when he was appearing at Irvings, he was undecided as to whether he was going to make the grade as a drag artiste, and he didn't tell his family and many of his friends until he was established to his own satisfaction. During that period he had some difficulty in keeping hidden the mounting wardrobe of female attire but, like most of the things he has set his mind on, he managed it.

Often, Victor Spinetti recalls, Danny's spontaneous humour

showed itself at the most unexpected times. Once, during his first appearance at a club, Danny took the wrong stairway when he made his exit and found himself in the kitchen. 'Hallo', he said to the surprised kitchen staff, crossed himself and went back up the stairs to find his dressing room.

In common with many drag artistes he often did two jobs at once, doubling with daytime work and club engagements in the evenings. In those early days Danny, while appearing in West End clubs late at night, appeared also at Stratford, East London, at one period for almost two years. It was hard work, a formidable training ground but Danny was convinced that he would make the top one day and that ambition kept him going when things were difficult. And even then he was never satisfied with anything but the best – his costumes, his wigs, the settings, the band – everything was rehearsed (if he could manage it) until it was all as perfect as he could make it. That continual striving for perfection is one of the hallmarks of professionalism in the often depressing, disappointing, uncertain and insecure world of the 'struggling' entertainer.

During those years at Churchills and Winstons Danny began to perform annually in pantomime for the late and great theatrical manager, Tom Arnold, who produced over three hundred revues and musical shows, including the Ivor Novello series, spectacular and original Ice Shows and major pantomimes each Christmas in the principal provincial cities throughout Britain. Danny always seemed to bring a new dimension to any part he played. Who else would have thought of portraying an Ugly Sister in pantomime as a modern blond?

But then he admits that his gimmick is to be as attractive as possible, even in unattractive parts. Danny's Ugly Sisters were ugly within but not on the outside, which probably makes them seem all the more wicked. Besides, as Danny has said more than once: 'if you can get real good belly laughs looking beautiful, why try to get them by dropping your drawers or having custard pies in your face?' Why indeed.

Danny's partner in the ugly sister routine in fourteen pantomimes was Alan Haynes, an artiste of rare and individual talent who also went on to have his own night club in London's West End. He has combined the qualities of glamour girl and traditional dame in many accomplished performances and occasionally he and Danny team up again as they did for the Christmas 1973 television performance of *Queen of Hearts* with Danny in the title role and Alan as the Queen Mother.

Yet, after what has been described as ten years' unbroken West End success, when Danny eventually confided that he had decided to take his personal act out of London, he was told that it couldn't be done! Up to 1956 he never earned more than £20 a week but now things were looking up and he could see that he must make a break with London clubs and be completely independent if he was ever to make a real name for himself.

The doubts in the minds of his friends and those who had his professional welfare and career at heart caused him to hesitate, but not for long. It was not the first time that he had tried something new or acted against advice, so with some apprehension he went to Margate, and broke all box-office records.

Over the years he had gradually but very successfully built up a valuable and essential asset for a public entertainer: a devoted and personal following that has grown with time. When he was playing night clubs for less than twenty pounds a week, Danny spent all he could on new clothes for the act and often went hungry. He was told by well-meaning friends that he was mad, but he hated 'tat' and felt that the road to success lay in his being as immaculate as possible in his stage presentation, and indeed off-stage as well. He has admitted that the glamorous women of the 1950s, people like Sabrina, Diana Dors, Elizabeth Taylor and Lady Docker, have influenced and contributed to his act.

Fellow artists, show business people he had come to know, and all his friends said, in effect, that he was fine for night clubs, variety shows and the occasional pantomime but he would never be able to hit the heights, unless he changed his act. After all, it was pointed out to Danny, time after time, no man had ever become a top star in a frock. But Danny knew that he was right and they were wrong. He used to reply that he didn't wear frocks, he wore costumes. He has always felt there is a big difference and he continued to add to his wardrobe, little thinking that the day would come when he would wear a two thousand pound Folies-style costume. Designed by delightful and talented Mark Canter, like most of his costumes these days, Danny wore this dream of beaded pink lace with a train that seemed almost to fill the stage in the 'Ta-ra-da-boom-de-ai' number in *Danny La Rue at The Palace* in 1970. It comprised five hundred feathers, graduated, dyed, and sewn on by hand. In his hair he wore ostrich plumes and on his arms, pearls and brilliants. Today his wardrobe is worth many thousands of pounds.

A little more serious than the revue and variety work that he had been doing and something of a milestone in his career, Danny starred in the original musical comedy *Come Spy With Me* at the Whitehall Theatre in 1966 and 1967; the theatre with rose-tinted mirrors that has seen so many successful Brian Rix productions. Danny's role as a spy enabled him to appear in a remarkable number of impersonations; changing his costume and his manner a dozen times. His 'Modesty Blaise – Barbarella' figure in skin-tight black plastic invariably received a great ovation in the show. The cast also included Barbara Windsor, Richard Wattis and Jackie Sands, who after training as a ballet dancer, had decided to make the musical theatre her career. She has appeared in many shows with Danny including the 1968 summer season at Margate and, in 1969, the record-breaking new pantomime *Queen Passionella and The Sleeping Beauty* at the Saville Theatre.

While he was appearing in *Come Spy With Me* an original portrait of Danny by Australian-born artist, Mary Talbot, was shown at the Trafford Gallery in Mount Street, London, and on 4 April 1967 Danny visited the gallery and was photographed in front of the delicate double portrait showing Danny three-quarters facing and also in profile surrounded by humming-birds, butterflies, fishes, leaves and flowers.

Victoria Mary Talbot now lives in Oslo and she met Danny briefly in London one evening after seeing his performance at Winstons Club in the summer of 1959. When she was again in London in 1967 a women friend mentioned that she had enjoyed *Come Spy With Me* very much and would like to meet Danny. This was arranged and then her friend asked Mary Talbot to paint a portrait of Danny. The artist thought over the idea and decided to try a full-face and profile using watercolours and coloured Indian ink. Later the picture was presented to Danny. After relating the story of the portrait to me Mary Talbot added: 'Danny is a sweet person and very modest and he makes people happy.'

His ability to make people happy is certainly one of the keys to Danny's success. 'Laughter, that's the thing,' he once told Peter Tipthorp. 'The best job my shows do is to give people a good laugh. For a couple of hours it takes them away from their problems and frustrations. That's marvellous. It always gives me a kick to think people want to see me. I think one of my assets is that I like people and when I'm on stage it shows.'

Not that he likes people in his dressing-rooms when he is preparing for a show. That is a different and very private matter. No outsider has witnessed Danny's complete transformation ritual and he feels that parts of it (dressed in female clothes but without a wig, for example) are frankly revolting. 'My costume is part of my act,' he said once. 'As a costume is to a clown. I don't get a kick out of wearing mine, as a transvestite might.'

In 1968 Danny starred in his own television special *An Evening with Danny La Rue;* he appeared in the 1968 Royal Television Show, and was the subject of several thought-provoking articles in newspapers and magazines. That year, an especially good one for Danny, also saw the release of his first record *On Mother Kelly's Doorstep,* his signature tune, and its climb into the popularity charts of the record business.

Also in 1968, he appeared as Queen Passionalla in *The Sleeping Beauty* at Golders Green. Talented Alan Haynes, who confidently combines the essential qualities of glamour and traditional pantomime dame, partnered Danny (as he had done many times before) and one of the hits of the show saw the two entertainers impersonate a number of current pop stars including Lulu, Sandie Shaw and Julie Felix; a more than superficial resemblence to the various artistes being cleverly achieved. For Danny the show meant thirty-four changes of costume.

The great success of these impersonations and such acts as Danny's impression of Julie Andrews in *The Sound of Music,* when he persuaded the children in the audience to join him on the stage for chorus after chorus of 'Do, ray, me', convinced Danny and his theatrical backers that there was West End potential in the idea and December 1969 saw the brilliant and very well received *Queen Passionella and The Sleeping Beauty* at the Saville Theatre, London (a theatre that opened in 1931 and closed in 1972) where it broke every known West End pantomime record.

Queen Passionella and The Sleeping Beauty took no less than two hundred and fifty thousand pounds at the box office and was a tremendous personal triumph for Danny who, by this time, was beginning to be used to success although this was something that even he had not dared to hope for.

Jackie Sands played 'Florizel' and Moya Donnelly the 'Sleeping Beauty'.

Meanwhile, in March 1964, Danny had opened (in partnership with David Lowes) his now legendry club in London's Hanover Square where he succeeded beyond his wildest dreams in extending the scope of his personal following and the club became the mecca of late-night entertainment.

At first many people thought Danny was mad when he said he was not going to have hostesses; instead he put on a brilliant and often gorgeous floor show. There were two bands, the food was good, the prices certainly not cheap but nobody was rooked. The club was an instant success and before long Danny was able to say that in sixteen years of show business he had never had a flop; he opened big and he always closed to capacity audiences; how many other top show business personalities can say the same thing?

'You've got to believe in yourself,' Danny says. 'Otherwise nobody will believe in you.' And to Danny's club came show people from Hollywood as well as Britain and personalities from most walks of life: Elizabeth Taylor, Bobby Moore, Billy Walker,

Freddie Trueman. Playwright Tennessee Williams was there one night and said it was the first time he had seen the point of a man dressing up as a woman. The club closed in March 1972 due to local property development.

Another performer in *Passionella* was David Ellen, a young man from Shoreham in Sussex (where Danny later owned a luxurious house). Ellen began his stage career as a dancer at the theatre with the best record for producing stars, the Windmill. He also appeared in summer shows and received his first big break in Scotland where he choreographed a number of shows. Returning to London in 1968 he appeared at Danny's club and after *Passionella,* appeared again with Danny in *The 1969 Birthday Show* at the Coventry Theatre, a show that virtually turned the city into a holiday town. Ellen went on to make a number of television appearances and he had a part in the film *Goodbye Mr Chips.* He also appeared in the 1969 Royal Variety Show at the London Palladium, in *Danny La Rue at the Palace,* the *Danny La Rue International Spectacular* at Blackpool in 1973 and the *Danny La Rue Show* at London's Prince of Wales Theatre 1973/4.

At the Danny La Rue Club, as indeed throughout his performances in drag, Danny's inner self barely pretended to be a woman at all. He always made a point of sending-up the female impersonation and leaving no doubt in the minds of his audience that he was a man. His first words always were, and still are, *'Wotcher, mates!'* and during his club performances, time and again he would leer, in the nicest possible way, at some pretty girl and

Above: A photograph by
David Steen of Danny in
the dressing room of his
legendary Hanover Square
club.

Right: Danny reproduced
every facet of the Bunny
Girl mystique in one of his
most famous routines at his
club.

Left: Danny with Ronnie Corbett at a rehearsal for the 1969 Royal Variety Show. Ronnie's eye had been injured in a car crash.

Left: Danny masquerades as an English rose for his night-club act.

Above: A typically lavish pantomime production. Danny with Alan Haynes.

Right: Danny (right) as a trendy blonde in a sketch with Alan Haynes, a memorable partnership.

Left: Danny as Lady Godiva in the Coventry Theatre Birthday Show, 1969.

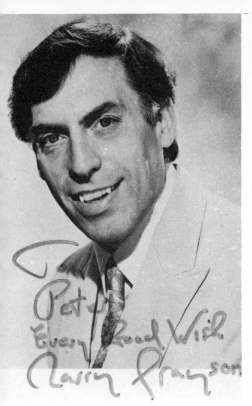

Larry Grayson: 'I did a drag
act for many years, but I
never liked those lashes and
wigs'.

Rex Jameson as the inimitable 'Mrs
Shufflewick'.

Right: Five famous 'Charlie's
Aunts' at the Apollo
Theatre, December 1970.
Back Row: Philip Dale,
Tom Courtenay (the latest
Charlie) and Leslie Phillips;
front: John Mills and
Danny.

say to the audience: 'Don't let the wig fool you, mate. . . ' And this emphasis on being 'a fella' explains to a large extent his great popularity among the sex he mimics in his performances.

By far the largest section of his devoted fans are women of mature years. I remember on one occasion counting the little crowd waiting to catch a glimpse of him at the stage door after a performance. There were four teenage girls and twenty-three women all over fifty. There is a certain pathos in his stage appearances and performance that appeals to the motherly instinct; a kind of little-boy-lost quality that many women find irresistible.

His entrances are carefully contrived and are invariably arresting. Often he sweeps into the spotlight in a long yellow satin dress, or something equally eye-catching, and after pausing for a moment to allow the illusion of glamour to have full effect, he opens with a most unladylike bawl: 'Wotcher, mates!' and from then on the show, and his club performances in particular can be very blue, is studded with reminders that he is a man with a man's feelings.

A similar ploy was used by the American, Van de Clyde Broodway, to open his sensational act that was tremendously popular between the two World Wars. Broodway worked under the name of Barbette and first dressed in female costume when he replaced a girl member of a trapeze act. He was so successful that he retained the female disguise for all his performances.

The opening sequence of Barbette's stage appearance in later years could almost have been a description of any leading female impersonator today. To the strains of tasteful music the curtain would rise on a setting of white curtains, a white carpet and white effects and, at the top of a silver staircase, Barbette would stand, immobile in a shimmering gown with a huge train. The sheer beauty of the presentation was breathtaking. After a few moments he would divest himself of the glittering head-dress and then the skirts and costume and go into his skilful trapeze act. The men in the audience would whistle and the women invariably loved him. He always took great trouble with his make-up and appearance, spending hours dressing and making-up for each performance; everything had to be perfect. He took his show all over Europe and was enjoying tremendous popularity when a fall during his act resulted in a stiff arm. Thereafter he choreographed and arranged trapeze routines for films and television.

Although Danny likes to think of himself as a 'huge fella', I am not certain that he is actually the 'six feet' he speaks of and certainly he is small-boned and really quite slight in build. He has expressive and well-cared for hands, not particularly effeminate but nice hands; tiny feet and huge beautiful brown eyes. His appearance is perhaps spoiled by his large mouth and the occasionally noticeable scar on the left side of his chin. He has remarkable teeth. He stands six feet one inch on stage and keeps physically fit and slim mainly from working. He likes good manners, hates rudeness and tries not to offend anyone.

Inevitably, and he knows it, the question in everyone's mind is how does he conceal his manhood. 'I know what you're thinking,' he said, during the course of an interview in 1970. 'I wonder where he puts it? Blimey, I've been doing this so long I just whistle and it goes away by itself! Mind you, it helps if it's cold outside!'

'Look,' he will tell you. 'I'm a man and when I go on stage you can see all the girls nudging each other and whispering has he or hasn't he?' So Danny has several gags to let the audience know that he knows what they're thinking. There's the one about his vital statistics: 'Well, let's say 38, 28, 38, 7. Yes, I'm a highly-strung girl!' Or maybe he's a beauty queen and when he is asked his measurements, he replies: '40, 26 and I wouldn't half make you jump!' Or he uses the 'whistle and it goes away on its own' routine and that always sets the audience roaring, and whistling.

There isn't really any secret about it. Many female impersonators wear a narrow belt in such a way that the penis and scrotum are drawn tightly backwards between the thighs. It is even possible for some men to hide their genitals by pushing them inside the body and taping them in that position; such female impersonators can then appear before an audience in a tight leotard, a tiny bikini or the briefest of underwear.

In stripping and less revealing acts failure to conceal the tell-tale bulge of a man is regarded in the profession as amateurish in the extreme. Some female impersonators believe they achieve the desired effect by wearing a tight girdle but most use a strap of rubber held taut between the legs by thin bands supported over the hips. Such an apparatus, called a 'gaff', holds the genitals tightly down and back between the legs.

During the course of an interview for *New Reveille* in 1973 Danny said: 'A bulge would be unsightly, so I wear a supertight jockstrap.' In this way the bulge is forced down between the legs and the 'fork' of the swimsuit lowered. 'In my last show,' went on Danny. 'I did an eighteen minute sequence in that jockstrap. It was sheer agony. The things I do for Bernard Delfont!'

After *The 1969 Birthday Show* (with Jackie Sands) – another record-breaker, this time at Coventry where the two thousand seat theatre was fully booked for the duration of the show, Danny appeared, looking somewhat embarrassed and uncomfortable as Lady Godiva for eight weeks in 'A Tribute to Coventry' that began on 15 October 1969 – came the most flattering event of his life so far for Danny. He was chosen to take part in the Royal Variety Show at the London Palladium in November 1969; an honour that was to be repeated in 1972.

At one point of that first Royal show Danny did the splits and he knew that those who had seen this part of his performance before were wondering whether he would look down at his crotch, as he usually did at that moment, and of course he did.

When he was presented afterwards it is said that the Queen tried to lure from Danny the secret of his quick costume changes, saying with a smile, 'It could be a help to me.'

There is a curious honesty about Danny that causes fellow-entertainers to say to him, very often: 'My God, you do get away with a lot.' But Danny says he has never been frightened of saying something that he thought he ought to say, and if there is anything of him in any of his characters, he thinks it's in the indestructible and forthright Lady Cynthia Grope, the dizzy female who makes pointed comment on leading political figures of the day.

The 1969 television presentation of *Charley's Aunt* with Danny in the lead was watched by an audience estimated at thirteen-and-a-half million. He played the part with gusto and his usual professional perfection but for many viewers it was not an altogether successful experiment. His name is so firmly linked in the public mind with exquisite female impersonation that it is going to be very difficult indeed for him to be accepted as anything else; a point that was again apparent in the reception given to his film, *Our Miss Fred.*

In the same year this indefatigable worker was guest-starred in the *Noel Coward Spectacular* and an edition of *Frost on Sunday* and he was voted Showbusiness Personality by the Variety Club of Great Britain.

On 9 April 1970, *Danny La Rue at the Palace* opened at the Palace Theatre, in the presence of Lord Snowdon and Princess Margaret and ran for over two years, although it was originally planned to run for one year. It cost some eighty thousand pounds to stage and reportedly grossed more than £1,400,000. After the opening charity show, which raised three thousand pounds for the Invalid Children's Aid Association, the Royal couple went backstage and met Danny and for the first time talked to him in drag. Lord Snowdon said he was especially impressed with Danny's impersonation of Marlene Dietrich; he had met and photographed this remarkable and unique entertainer and he was quite taken aback by the likeness when Danny came on.

Yet in one way Danny does not impersonate women sincerely or exactly. Critic Ronald Bryden hit the nail on the head when he said, 'He's like some giant doll . . the essence of the joke being not to pass himself off as a woman, but to dress up as a larger-than-life model of the sex.'

With a seating capacity of over fourteen hundred the three-tier Palace Theatre at Cambridge Circus opened in 1891 as the Royal English Opera House under the management of Richard D'Oyly Carte who planned the building as a home for English Opera. With the collapse of D'Oyly Carte's hopes and ambitions for English opera, and a Sarah Bernhardt season, the theatre changed hands and became the Palace Theatre of Varieties in 1892. There Marie Tempest made her first appearance; Pavlova made her London debut there and for a time it was the venue of the Royal Command Variety Performances.

After a short season as a cinema in 1920, Charles B Cockran ran *The Op-timists* for a long season at the theatre. The original versions of *No, No, Nanette* and *The Girl Friend* ran at The Palace, the former for six hundred and fifty-five performances from March 1925 and the latter for four hundred and twenty-one performances from September 1927. In the early 1940's the theatre became the home of the Jack Hulbert and Cicely Courtneidge musical comedies and in 1949 Ivor Novello composed and starred in *King's Rhapsody* which achieved eight hundred and thirty-nine performances before the tragic death of Ivor in 1951. In more recent years the theatre has seen such talented performers as Norman Wisdom in *Where's Charley?* (based on *Charley's Aunt*) and Laurence Olivier in *The Entertainer* and such modern productions as *Hair*.

When the new musical was announced in February 1970 it was reported that *Danny La Rue at the Palace* was just one of two shows Danny would be appearing in under a new three-year contract which could bring him as much as £500,000 if one included the earnings from his London night club. Described as 'an adult entertainment' the cast of *Danny La Rue at The Palace* included Roy Hudd, Toni Palmer, David Ellen and Jackie Sands. Roy Hudd was encouraged by Michael Bentine to try the stage as a career. Bentine spotted the original talent in the young comedian and after a season at Butlin's Holiday Camp at Clacton, Roy Hudd appeared in variety, Shakespeare, films, pantomime, television, Talk of the Town and his own television show. A dedicated performer who has worked hard for his success, his only ambition is 'to stay in this fascinating business until I'm too old to totter on to the stage; that, for me,' he says, 'would be happiness.' *At the Palace* was Roy Hudd's first musical in London's West End.

Toni Palmer began her stage career as a dancer in the big American musicals at the Coliseum Theatre in memorable shows such as *Kiss Me Kate, Guys and Dolls* and *Can-Can*. She was also in the West End production of *Fings Ain't Wot They Used T'be* and she had a leading role in Lionel Bart's *Blitz*. She became popular when she was one of the original girls in the television series *The Rag Trade* and more television and film work followed as well as parts in plays at the Yvonne Arnauld Theatre, Guilford and London's Mermaid Theatre.

Danny La Rue at The Palace (described by one American commentator as 'the hottest thing in town') was written by Barry Cryer and Dick Vosburgh with original music and lyrics by Bill Solly and special material by Bryan Blackburn. Barry Cryer has contributed innumerable scripts and patter for Danny and at one time he worked with him as 'feed' at his club. Among the stars he has written for are David Frost, Max Bygraves, Tommy Cooper and Morecombe and Wise. Lionel Blair staged and wrote parts of the production which was directed by Freddie Carpenter who began his association with Danny when he staged *Queen Passionella and The Sleeping Beauty;* since then he has directed all Danny's shows. A native of Australia (where he was working when I was researching this book) he directed Anna Neagle 'down under' in *Charlie Girl* and Cyd Charisse and subsequently Yvonne de Carlo in *No, No, Nanette;* and more recently, Moira Lister in *Cowardy Custard* in South Africa.

At the Palace was elaborately staged, beautifully dressed and so colourful and popular that it was difficult to obtain tickets throughout the two-year run. Like all his shows by this time it

was unashamedly a vehicle for Danny and his exuberance
pervaded the whole lavish show. Whether he was masquerading as
Fanny Oakley, Lady Cynthia Grope, a well-proportioned Mrs UK
in a Mrs World 1970 sketch, raising the roof with
'Ta-ra-da-boom-de-ai' or his finale 'Salute to the Stars', it was a
glamorous and enjoyable musical event that drew parties in their
hundreds from every part of the country.

Throughout the long run Danny said he felt scared every single
time before he went on stage. There were fifteen hundred people
waiting and he has always had a feeling when performing that it
was 'either them or you'. They were half-way on your side
because they had come to see you but you still had to impose
your will on them, a frightening and at the same time, a
fascinating thing to do; a challenge if you like and challenges
Danny likes. He accepted the challenge and won at each and every
performance and for Danny *At the Palace* was another huge
success. He never gets bored going on stage day after day. 'How
can you?' he asks. 'When you are doing the thing you like best of
all.'

His name had by now become a household word practically
without the aid of television, radio or records, although he had
worked in all three media. At last his remarkable talents,
incredible hard work and warm stage personality paid off as never
before. Even Danny found it difficult to believe. 'Twenty-five
months at the Palace with insurance premiums at £260 a week,
the highest ever known' he said afterwards. 'I feel like a no-claim

car: no bumps after two years!' The insurance was reduced after twelve months.

Years before, the Palace Theatre had seen another original and outstanding female impersonator, an American named Julian Eltinge, to whom, whether he knows it or not, Danny owes a great deal. Eltinge originated the idea that a female impersonator could be glamorous and he proved that such an occupation could be a full-time legitimate career.

He raised impersonation from the drab female garb of music hall turns to beautiful transformations with the accent on charm and delicacy. His shows, like Danny's, were all conceived especially for him and tailored to his particular talents; although nearly all used the theme that a man had to disguise himself as a woman and his acts included such titles as 'The Fascinating Widow', 'Countess Charming' and, by way of variation, 'Her Grace the Vampire'.

After his Broadway début in 1904, Eltinge came to London in 1906 and had an outstanding success at the Palace Theatre. He also gave a command performance for King Edward VII at Windsor Castle. Until Eltinge's act there was no real artistry in drag performances but he set a new standard by presenting a completely new approach to an art that has flourished ever since, to reach full flower with Danny La Rue. Eltinge set the drag scene on its feet by exploiting the glamorous side of impersonation. It will be interesting to see whether the example of Eltinge's later life is followed by Danny. A respected figure of the theatrical establishment, Eltinge retired at the age of forty-six, after about thirty years on the stage, to live in a spectacular and luxurious house. Ten years later he made a come-back.

The great difference between the two entertainers lies in the fact that while Danny's night club shows and to a lesser extent all his appearances, are undoubtedly *risqué,* even bawdy; Julian Eltinge was purity itself; his patter never even touched on sexual themes. That aspect apart, there is a great similarity between the two performers, even to physical resemblances including the fine hands, twinkling eyes, a frank and open grin, punctiliousness in dress and make-up, and a considerable sex appeal and fascination for older women.

By the time it closed *Danny La Rue at the Palace* had been seen by no fewer than 1,200,000 people. The management claimed it could have run for another five years and they were reported to be almost sobbing (on their way to the bank) as they turned away customers and put up the 'Closed' notice. And still, every night, all through the run at the Palace, Danny appeared at his own Hanover Square club. It was also in 1970 that Danny was voted Theatre Personality of the Year by the Gallery First-Nighters, an honour he deeply appreciated. He was also the subject of an unsigned profile in the American edition of *Vogue* dated 1 September, 1970, illustrated with two photographs by Lord Snowden, one, full-page, of Danny in drag and the other as he looks off-stage. Describing him as 'wildly magnificent'. . . 'spike-fingered' . . . and with 'swoop gestures', the piece tells of him sharing a house with his mother at Hampstead at that time; driving nightly to the Palace Theatre and then on to his club, often getting only four hours sleep but, says the article, the grind suits him and he saves the money apart from 'a few obvious luxuries like owning three cars and part of three greyhounds and a racehorse.'

The American view of Danny at this period is interestingly presented. 'When La Rue steps into the spotlight, awash in satin, a crazy, bawdy, allure takes over. He makes swipes at women that no other man or woman could get away with . . in drag his curiously mechanical walk, his rococo disguises that appear and disappear with kaleidoscopic swiftness, his deep-indigo jokes, his top-drawer characters, are delivered with a wide, mocking grin and a wink at the audience . . . '

Within months of the Palace show closing Danny was appearing in his sixteenth pantomime, *Queen of Hearts* at the Palace Theatre, Manchester, where the run had to be extended by four weeks to meet the demand for tickets. It was the scene of his first pantomime triumph.

A specially adapted version of the *Queen of Hearts* was recorded at the New Theatre, Oxford, and shown on television on Christmas Day 1973. In a typically colourful and fast-moving spectacular Danny managed to appear in twelve dazzling costumes which varied from one that looked as though it was made from thousands of butterfly wings to a slinky orange dress worth all of two thousand pounds and trimmed with a thousand pound's worth of fur. Altogether the costumes, specially designed for the pantomime, cost over ten thousand pounds.

The show was recorded during the course of one thirteen-hour day which included two full-length rehearsals and a final camera recording before an audience. The cast included Peggy Mount and Alan Haynes – he and Danny have done fourteen pantomimes together – and his vivid orange dressing-gown at the eleven o'clock rehearsal contrasted with Danny's flowery silk wrap. As soon as Danny appeared an order buzzed round the Theatre: 'No photographs of Mr La Rue until he is properly dressed.' 'I'm like a magician who doesn't want to give away his secrets,' laughed Danny. 'But why should I let the illusion be destroyed?'

Gradually the rehearsal moved forward to the highlight of the show and the inevitable slapstick comedy scene in the palace bakery, complete with custard tarts. In an effort to preserve the floor and Danny's carefully made-up face, this particular part of the rehearsal was conducted in slow-motion mime without the custard tarts. For at least one person present (Peter Genower of *TV Times*) it was almost better than the real thing.

After lunch the full dress rehearsal began. Danny, who wore each costume a mere seven-and-a-half minutes, disappeared off-stage time and again and reappeared almost miraculously in a different outfit. For others in the cast the final rehearsal did not do as well. Peggy Mount lost her enormous hat twice; a girl dancer fell as she pranced into the wings and more than one of those taking part swore they would give up the stage, before the rehearsal was through, and then almost without realisation, the whole cast discovered that the effect of that trying rehearsal had been to wind up the entire company for the evening recording.

Back in his dressing room Danny relaxed with a cup of tea ('I need this for my throat; usually I drink Buck's Fizz during a show but we're in and out of here today so I haven't bothered to get any in'). For such an extended show Danny doesn't bother to remove his make-up; after all it takes him nearly an hour to put it on in the morning and after that he does what he calls a 're-touching job' here and there; 'painting in bits and sharpening it up.' Fortunately he does not need to shave more than once a day although in any case he uses theatrical make-up which is thick enough to cover any stubble. He says he could grow a beard in a week.

Danny's reluctance to admit that some of his jokes are very blue is evident from his comment on a take-off of Fanny Cradock in the bakery slapstick scene, when he has Fanny saying: 'Girls, are you having trouble with your dumplings? Does your old man wake up in the night and fancy a little cracker?' 'Innuendo?' asks Danny, his eyes wide with innocence. 'What innuendo? Blue is in the eye of the beholder.'

Eventually the recording went off without a hitch and at last Danny eased himself out of the last costume for the last time since those particular gowns would not be used again. He was asked what would happen to them. 'I give a lot away,' he replied. 'Or we strip the fur off, dye it again, and use it on another dress.'

As with all his recorded work, Danny made a point of watching the programme when it was broadcast. He spent the day at his hotel by the Thames and he put his feet up but he was alert and attentive as soon as the show began. 'You have to strive for perfection in this business,' he told Peter Genower, 'and you can only do that by watching yourself for mistakes, looking out for little things you can improve on and so on.'

Although he was busy in pantomime one Christmas not long ago he still found time to impersonate Father Christmas at the Variety Club of Great Britain's Christmas Lunch at the Dorchester Hotel where Mr Edward Heath, then Prime Minister, was guest of honour. It was a change to wear a beard after all those gorgeous wigs.

Since 1950 all of Danny's wigs have been supplied by Stanley Hall and the first wig he made for Danny was when the young entertainer was appearing at a basement theatre show in Panton Street. Even then Danny looked so good at night clubs that the chorus girls in the show seemed quite tatty beside him, Stanley Hall recalls. Danny's wigs, many of them containing forty thousand individual hairs that are sewn on at the rate of four hundred to the square inch, are mainly of human hair. The hair comes from Italian convents and consists of the shorn locks of nuns who have taken their final vows. It is bought by the sackfull and costs anything between five pounds and thirty pounds an ounce, depending on the quality and the colour; the fairer it is, the higher the price, for blondes are rare in Italy.

When Danny first bought wigs from Stanley Hall they cost about twenty pounds each; in fact Danny can remember when he used to buy the wigs on credit, some twenty years ago. 'I couldn't afford to pay for my wigs then but Stanley never worried about it. He thought that, given time, I might just make enough money to settle the bills!' Now most of Danny's wigs cost a hundred pounds or more since they have to stand up to considerable knocking about. Even so the wigs in Danny's shows are returned to Stanley Hall for re-dressing nearly every week. Many of the more extravagant styles are made from the cheaper Asian or yak's hair. Danny keeps thirty or forty wigs with him for every show and possesses a vast collection which he has accumulated over the years for, with wigs as with everything, he hates to throw them away.

In spite of his success Danny knew that the higher up the ladder you get in the entertainment world, the harder you have to strive. He said a few years ago: 'I could name a dozen good artistes who were at the top of the ladder once and now they are scraping for work: that frightens me.' But at least he had succeeded in the struggle to rise above most of the entertainers of his day and he was conscious that there was an equally strenuous struggle to stay at the top and that there would always be new heights to climb. Armed with these sobering thoughts Danny looked confidently ahead.

Part Five
The Results of
Success

ON JULY 27, 1970, DURING THE WEEK IN WHICH HE CELEBRATED HIS
forty-third birthday, Danny completed the purchase of The Swan
Inn, Streatley, Berkshire, a modernised eighteenth-century
Thames-side hotel for which he paid £100,000. Subsequent
improvements have probably doubled its value.

The land on both sides of the river was included in the sale and
also Hegmore Island, which has extensive tea-gardens and private
moorings. Danny said at the time, standing on the riverbank,
throwing chunks of bread to a couple of swans: 'By purchasing
The Swan I have fulfilled two long-standing ambitions. It has
long been my desire to operate a good country hotel and I've
always wanted to own an island.' Today Danny looks upon The
Swan as his pension, his security. He has seen so many people in
show business make a fortune and then lose it. If it all stopped
for Danny tomorrow, he'd still have The Swan and all it means to
him.

The Swan Inn, situated in the Goring Gap, one of the most
beautiful and renowned stretches of the Thames, boasts
twenty-eight bedrooms and has become tremendously popular as a
centre for holidaymakers, tourists and honeymooners. Danny once
reminded sceptical newspapermen who were used to seeing him
amid the bright lights of the entertainment world, that he had
always enjoyed the countryside; he loved Devon as a boy and had
hopes of returning there one day but in any case he said he
certainly planned to spend more and more time in the Berkshire
countryside in the future.

Occasionally, if you are lucky and the time is right, you might catch Danny singing a song for customers at The Swan; but it will be sung straight by a cheerful Irishman in male attire, probably sweater and slacks for he prefers casual clothes away from the stage or official engagements.

'I love it down here,' he told Peter Tipthorp of *Annabel* in 1973. 'Working so hard with all those feathers and tinsel, I need balance and solidarity. I find that here. To me there's nowhere in the world as nice. I'm Dan down here. No one makes a fuss, no one worries me. I'm a local chap. They think of me as a local. I went to one of the pubs in the village the other night to push over the pennies for a charity. I had a marvellous time.'

At The Swan Danny's friend Michael C Oxford became Managing Director, Jack Hanson (Danny's Personal Manager) Director, and Danny himself Chairman of 'The Swan Inn, Streatley, Limited'. By this time Danny also had a large house at Hampstead, another at Shoreham in Sussex, and one near Henley. He owned a Rolls, a Bentley and a Mercedes, a yacht, racehorses, greyhounds and had investments in a model agency. Later he bought a *château* in the south of France at a reported £100,000.

However, Danny was beginning to tire of dressing-up as a woman. He said, more and more often, that he would like to 'hang up his Bristols' (Bristol City = tittie). He appeared on stage in male clothes whenever the opportunity occurred and he was cautious about how and when he was viewed or photographed in full drag.

Apart from definite and acceptable stage engagements he was careful to ensure that his appearances in public were in immaculate male dress. During press interviews he emphasised the fact that his job began and ended on the stage; that he had two fully-mirrored dressing-rooms—one for himself and one for the costumes—and they didn't ever mix. He turned down opportunities to star in the roles of Dolly and Mame on Broadway (after a great deal of thought) on the grounds that the parts in *Hullo Dolly* and *Mame* (taking over from Janis Paige) were written for women. 'I could not go on as Mame and sing love songs to men,' he said. 'It would be against the way I feel;' and, more revealingly, he reportedly added: 'I don't like physical contact and I've never played in America and if I'm going to fall there it will be on my own terms and in my own show.'

'I'm pretty cool about the costumes,' he told Alix Coleman of *TV Times* in June 1972. 'If I liked wearing them too much I wouldn't be good at it.' The careful façade that he had built up for years was in danger of taking him over. It was Frankenstein all over again and Danny was not having it; not if he could help it.

He refused to be seen making up and he refused to appear in costume for television rehearsals. Even if the part he played was that of a woman, he would not wear the costumes until the final full dress rehearsal. He was lucky to get away with it. 'I let them see the clothes for lighting and colour, but I'm never in front of the cameras until I'm ready for the show.' The fact that he was permitted to dictate such terms shows just how much he was trusted. Everyone knew that on the night they could rely, utterly and completely, on Danny's performance.

He began to look at himself as others saw him. 'I quite understand that some people think it is peculiar for a fellow to dress as a tart; but I don't dress up because I like it. The reason I dress up is for laughs,' he says, emphasising that the dressing-up itself is unimportant; perhaps even attempting to convince himself during his rare moments of seriousness.

Apart from the exacting make-up and minutely accurate dressing-up, playing female roles was beginning to become very strenuous, physically and orally. He had to use various types of voice inflections for the different characters and, he says, 'basically I'm a baritone.' He has two dogs and tries to keep healthy and slim. He likes to think he has not lost contact with the workaday world and often points out during the course of interviews that he does more than pass the time of day with tradesmen. As he said to Sydney Edwards of the London *Evening Standard* in 1968: 'I know my milkman very well.'

More by way of justification than explanation he will tell you: 'It has taken me twenty years to make something that wasn't acceptable, accepted; and I'm still learning all the time . . . I mean, it's not funny to put on a frock and wig; it's just not funny. It takes a lot of time to develop a character that is inoffensive and can be played to all age groups.'

While never pretending (these days) to be anything more than a rib-nudging, winking and hip-shaking imposter, his impersonations are still initially impressive by virtue of the sheer accuracy and thoroughness of his personification of the women he represents. With almost unbelievable exactitude he mirrors not only the minute details of how women walk, pause, sit down, look at a man, hold a handbag, touch their hair or dress, glance at their fingernails or their feet, flicker their eyelashes or wrinkle their noses but he has also mastered, and can project in some indefinable way, the panache that lifts the impersonation out of the classification of mere caricature and consequently his characterisations remain feminine without ever seeming effeminate. It is this special quality of observation and personification that allows women to accept and enjoy his act with its underlying suggestion that he knows what they think and feel to a truly remarkable degree.

This carefully created and glamorous creature is often shattered within seconds. Danny explained once that when the (apparently) gorgeous creature comes onto the stage, the audience gasps; but once that is over he has to do something more so he shatters her with his stage voice, gruff and deep, a voice that a street vendor might envy. He has conquered the art of wearing female costume without flaunting or showing off, which would be common and distasteful. Danny always appears elegantly dressed and usually keeps well within the boundaries of the character he is portraying.

Much of what he does these days Danny has filmed. During the run of *Danny La Rue at the Palace* he watched every scene many

times until he was satisfied that it couldn't be bettered. He
considers himself to be his best critic and sometimes tapes shows
and the audience reaction over a period of weeks, listening
carefully to the laughter and where it comes. Then he alters his
timing, his pauses and his intonation until he feels it can't be
improved any more. He says he never forgets that eighty per cent
of his audience are ordinary families and they have to watch what
they spend. 'You can't be *blasé* with them. They're not gullible.
Well, yes,' he admits. 'It is aggression, used constructively.'

He loves performing. 'I'm mad – I'm stage-struck,' he says, his
eyes bright and half-smiling. 'I'm not ashamed of saying that I
love the theatre and I like to think of the audience as a big party,'
is the kind of thing he says and one never quite knows how
sincere he is for he does attend parties, both private ones with
friends and public ones, when he is very much the successful
entertainer looking for the limelight.

He is in great demand wherever beautiful girls are to be found.
In November 1970 he was a guest of honour when the Variety
Club of Great Britain *fêted* the Miss World beauty contest finalists
at a luncheon at the Savoy Hotel. In November 1971 he was a
guest with Stanley Baker and Roger Moore, with Earl
Mountbatten as guest of honour, when the Variety Club
entertained the 1971 Miss World contestants. In April 1973 he
was at Thames TV studio in London when the 1973 Miss TV
Times semifinals were held. He asked what all the girls were
doing and when told replied: 'They don't stand a chance, do

they!' One of the ten girls selected for the finals was Miss Carla Wansey-Jackson of Haslemere, the current Miss Farnham, and I asked her for details of the encounter. She told me that the meeting with Danny was incredibly brief but she noted, even in those few seconds, that he appeared 'in the flesh' exactly as he looks on the stage or screen: a handsome, well-turned-out individual who would naturally gain a second look in the street. She also gained the impression that he was a genuine person and very popular, not just the type of popularity that comes with fame. He seemed to be on good terms with the TV crews and the ladies, joking as four of the girls passed but yet he was very polite and professional.

Although a deeply religious man, a practising Roman Catholic, Danny is broadminded. 'If someone likes reading porn, then that's their kick,' he told *TV Times* in 1972; and he sees nothing dirty in anyone doing what they want to do. During an act he can be blue to the point of obscenity and his late-night audiences usually love it – although there are those who have fallen asleep during his act and others who have left the theatre in protest – but off-stage you will never hear him tell a blue joke.

He told Dennis Holman of *New Reveille* that he has a built-in audience meter; three gags by which he can judge how people are going to react to his brand of blue humour and he recounted one gag, written for him by Denis Norden: 'To the pure all things are pure. Did you hear the latest about Mary Whitehouse? She switched on the radio, heard a voice say ". . . tits like coconuts," and switched off and telephoned the BBC. "It was absolutely disgusting," she told the producer. "Madam," he replied. "If you hadn't switched off you would have also heard . . . and sparrows like breadcrumbs." '

Danny feels that the essence of any blue material is timing and timing he is very good at. 'If you sit on it, it becomes vulgar. It must be sat on and then right off. Then it becomes a giggle.' Well, it's a point of view and Danny has certainly conquered the art of putting across objectionable material unobjectionably. 'I am a bit naughty,' he says and likes to refer to himself as 'Max Miller in sequins, the Cheeky Chappie in a frock.' 'People expect me to be naughty and I am,' he told Peter Tipthorp. 'I aim at being *risqué* but if a gag is offensive, I'll kill it at once.'

He says English people like fruity material but not blue jokes. 'English people are very clean-minded. Only dirty people think of dirty jokes.' He's clever enough to tell people exactly what they want to hear. 'I don't think dirty at all,' he says, 'at any time.'

He admits that his shows are bawdy – or cheeky, as he calls them – but there is no pornography, he insists. 'In one scene,' he told Dennis Holman, 'I literally put my hands inside Toni Palmer's swimsuit and feel her breasts, but there's nothing dirty about that. Just fun. Porn, almost by definition, can't be funny.'

'What makes people laugh?' he will ask and before you have time to reply, gives his answer: 'Words – the gag.' In one part of his act he'll be wearing a maxi overcoat and he'll start trying to undo the buttons at the back. He gets into the kind of heated muddle that only he can get into and then he turns round and apologises to the man behind him, saying he is embarrassed. 'So am I, love,' the man replies. 'You've undone four of mine!'

Even the corniest material is used, if Danny thinks it is funny, such as the sketch when he goes into a chemist shop and asks for some talcum powder and the man says, 'Walk this way.' Danny replies, with a flutter of his eyelids, 'If I walked that way, chum, I wouldn't need the talcum powder.' It is all a matter of timing because that is the excitement of the theatre. Danny likes to quote Charles Coburn, 'who summed it all up when he said, "You've got to make them think you're bloody marvellous." '

Different people view Danny's performances in different ways, which is as it should be. Some regard his material and his presentation as vulgar and unjustifiable, pandering to the lowest taste; rather more feel that his particular presentation takes away the dirty snigger and they can laugh openly at words and phrases which, if they were said to them by the man next door, they would consider an insult; but within the shelter of the theatre and with Danny's innocent eyes upon them, they can laugh and enjoy themselves. The vast majority of Danny's audience, however, are broadminded themselves and accept that there is humour in everything and especially in every activity between men and women.

He loves playing to children and then he is more careful. Even in pantomime he may 'edge it up' at night when there are only a few children present but at *matinée* performances when the theatre is full of youngsters he is, as he puts it, 'not my usual sort of funny at all.' Here perhaps one glimpses again the real artiste; sensing his audience and giving them what they will most understand, appreciate and enjoy; and always with a charm and underlying kindness and thoughtfulness that denotes the true professional entertainer.

Danny is very fond of children. He sometimes talks of getting married one day for he would certainly like to have a couple of children and anyway he does not visualise retirement on his own. 'I'd probably be a possessive husband,' he told one reporter. 'But I would be very understanding.'

Meanwhile he has a favourite niece and he never misses an opportunity of helping unfortunate children. In May 1972 he donated two of the Variety Club of Great Britain's 'sunshine' coaches for handicapped children. Afterwards he was photographed, accompanied by his mother, with the Duke of Edinburgh who inspected the coaches. They are of special construction to ensure the safety and comfort of handicapped children passengers and each coach cost two thousand pounds. These particular coaches were presented by Danny to Borocourt Hospital, Wyfold, Reading and Wayland Hospital, Bradfield, Berkshire.

Danny says that on stage he is sexless and he feels that all true artistes should be sexless during their acts. This may be another facet of his characterisations that makes him acceptable to such a wide audience. He maintains that nobody has ever come up to him and said, 'I think you're bleeding disgusting' (to be honest they'd have a job to get near him) and that he has never had a 'peculiar' letter. When one considers that a girl modelling underclothes or a bikini in a newspaper or magazine probably receives many letters from dirty old men, this fact suggests that Danny gets across to his audience, in a really remarkable way, his sincerity, sense of fun, and the impression that he is 'all right'.

Of course he does get some letters that amuse him. After he did a half-price *matinée* for old-age pensioners, a WVS woman wrote to say that she thought he would be amused at part of a conversation she had overheard between two old ladies at the show, when he had worn a lurex dress. One said, 'Did you watch him when he walked? It was like a racehorse.' And the other replied: 'Yes, and I wish I had one of those shiny Durex dresses like he was wearing!'

Another letter came from a woman who said she had had a breast removed because of cancer but she saw the humour of Danny's Mae West act where he wears a rubber bosom and says, in an aside to the audience: 'They're like Dunlop, thirty thousand miles and still going strong . . .' Yet there was an undercurrent of sadness in the letter for the writer said she was embarrassed at having only one breast and asked for Danny's help. He suggested she went to see a local theatrical costumier; a thoroughly practical suggestion that might not have occurred to anyone but Danny.

Jack Hanson, Danny's manager, tells me that Danny gets a lot of requests for personal appearances for charity and he accepts as often as he can although such appearances have to fit in with his professional engagements but he frequently officiates at such events as the Kensington Antiques Fair. He opened the twentieth Fair at Kensington Town Hall on 14 October, 1971 and was pictured afterwards playing with an automatic French (or possibly German) drum-playing bear dating from 1750 and valued at £500. As always his appearance was a great success. Among the unusual honours that have come his way is the Honorary Presidency of the London School of Economics Students' Union.

He has received many offers from companies who want him to promote their products but he has yet to make his first 'commercial'. He feels that he has a responsibility to his public in this respect and is determined to be very careful before he puts his name to any commercial product. At one time he seriously considered doing a man's hair-spray advertisement but after trying the commodity he decided against it, or as he politely puts it, 'the idea fell through.'

It is often said that Danny La Rue made female impersonation successful and accepted and that he, more than anyone, is responsible for the drag acts that have become popular pub entertainment, not only in London but throughout the country. Another point of view suggests that in fact he made himself respectable and accepted, and rose from the mediocrity of the drag cult to the established and legitimate theatre impersonation act. Whatever happened it is the name of Danny La Rue that immediately comes to mind whenever female impersonation is mentioned today.

And yet, female impersonation and drag artistes have existed as long as the theatre. One of the oldest forms of stage shows, the Kabuki Theatre of Japan, has always had an all-male cast with highly esteemed actors playing female parts, a situation depicted in the Contemporary Films production, *An Actor's Revenge.* So it has been throughout history. In Tudor times, in England, women were not permitted to appear on the stage and consequently all plays at that time, including Shakespeare's works, had youths playing the female roles. This has been tried again, with varying degrees of success, in recent years: one recalls the National Theatre production of *As You Like It* in 1967. Conversely such actresses as Sarah Bernhardt and Esmé Beringer have played the title role in productions of *Hamlet.* China too has a long history of female impersonation, originating in the reign of Ch'ien Lung (1735-1796) when the authorities banned the appearance of women on the stage for moral reasons. In fact one of the greatest female impersonators of all time was Chinese and it is interesting to recall a little of the career of Mei Lan-Fang and to compare him with Danny La Rue.

Born in 1894, Mei Lan-Fang always claimed that hard work made him the idol of China. In 1924 he was voted the most popular actor in the country and he received many honours. He toured extensively and his charm and talent were admired by all who met him. He perfected new examples of artistic expression, created plays and shows for himself, made films, and his artistry and original presentation were copied by other impersonators.

In the Western world *Charley's Aunt* is a perennial stage presentation that relies on a man taking to female dress because of circumstances in the plot. Over the years the setting of the play has changed from the Edwardian era to a modern version for television; with Danny playing the title role as a seductive temptress, a version and characterisation that was praised by some critics and viewers but disliked by others.

Danny himself was delighted to have the opportunity to play the part because he felt that the character was balanced between the real Danny and 'the bird'. He is always pleased these days when he can appear as himself, a fact that could account for his innumerable public appearances, always in male attire. Today Danny feels that he is a good actor and he would like to try something in the Brian Rix style or one of the Georges Feydeau farces that Patrick Cargill does so well.

Although Danny cannot really see himself as a straight actor, he is fascinated by the realisation that if comedy is difficult to perform, farce is twice as difficult. Comedy Danny is good at, now he would like to try farce. But he has no illusions about being a really great star. 'That's another dimension – the indefinable "it," ' he once said. 'Garland, Chevalier, Dietrich, that's the "it" quality and I haven't got it – yet!' There are members of his audience and those of his devoted following who would not agree and believe that Danny has indeed that indefinable something that makes a really great star.

A few years ago there was a suggestion that Danny would make an interesting Millamant in *The Way of the World,* Congreve's masterpiece of compressed and witty dialogue that is a subtle exploration of the morality of sex among the characters who regard it more as a weapon for intimidation and a currency for bribes than a pleasure between lovers. Nothing came of the idea. Perhaps someone recalled the failure of William Douglas Home's play *Aunt Edwina* in 1959. Henry Kendall, actor, director, revue and pantomime dame of renown, played the army colonel who changed sex. Transvestism, like convincing drag, is something of a rarity on the stage. A notable exception was Simon Gray's play *Wise Child* that starred Sir Alec Guinness; a play that included also two homosexual characters but again, it was not altogether successful commercially although Sir Alec gave a memorable performance in his portrayal of a minor crook who adopts drag as a disguise. In fact, he was only seen out of drag during the final five minutes of the play.

In my contact with the bewildering and often unreal world of show business, seeking material for this book, I was often told that transvestism is rife among drag artistes but Danny is no transvestite; he is only too keen to discard ladies' costumes and wear male clothing whenever he can and indeed he would like nothing better than never to wear women's clothing again; something he has recently threatened to do. After all it has been a long time now but while he retains the undoubted popularity that he has enjoyed in recent years, it will be understandable if he should continue, especially since the theatre and all it stands for, means so much to him.

Incidentally transvestism of an unusual kind is evident in the immortal Barrie play, *Peter Pan*, for the real sex of the principal part is never revealed although when the play has been performed annually at Christmas in London 'Peter' is always played by a young actress. It has been suggested that girls in the audience fall in love with 'Peter' and for the boys, he becomes a hero; later when the boys grow up and take their own children to see the play, they fall in love with the youthful and attractive 'Peter', thereby continuing the unending chain of adulation for the unattainable.

Some people have reservations about Danny's over-exposure on television in recent years, his endless appearance at parties and private functions, and in particular his film *Our Miss Fred,* which was not a success. Instead, it has been suggested that he should be persevering with becoming a legend, something he was well on the way to achieving in the late 1960s. On the other hand his appearances, in almost any capacity, are invariably an enormous success and a case in point was the 1972 Switch-On of Blackpool's Illumination Display, an event that has earned the title of 'the greatest free show on earth'.

Robert S Battersby, Blackpool's Director of Attractions and Publicity, was very helpful when I approached him for some details and he told me that while previous switch-on ceremonies have been carried out by eminent personalities from all walks of

life, including Anna Neagle, Sir Stanley Matthews, George
Formby, Jayne Mansfield and Gracie Fields, none of them excelled
the tremendous impact which Danny made upon the huge crowds
that gathered to watch him perform the six hundred thousand
pound Diamond Jubilee celebration of the occasion (the first-ever
display of lights in Blackpool took place in 1912) although, due
to the intervention of two World Wars, the 1972 display was not
in fact the sixtieth.

Nevertheless, Robert Battersby tells me, the Blackpool Council
felt that someone of outstanding reputation and if possible 'with a
glittering personality' (that would match the Diamond Jubilee
Switch-On) must be found for this special occasion. They found
that person in Danny La Rue, 'a charming and very likeable man,'
and when they discovered that he was going to fulfil one of his
lifelong ambitions by appearing in his own show for a Blackpool
Summer Season in 1973, they knew they had made an ideal
choice.

During negotiations (Danny interrupted a holiday in the South
of France following the conclusion of his film *Our Miss Fred* to
attend the function) Blackpool Council arranged with the Minister
for Aerospace and the British Aircraft Corporation, a public
showing of Concorde 002 by means of a flight over Blackpool on
Friday, 8 September, the night of the switch-on. As soon as this
was fixed the Council began to consider the possibility of linking
these historic events in the life of Blackpool.

The actual Switch-On Ceremony takes place traditionally from a huge dais in front of the Town Hall in Talbot Square late in the evening of the first Friday in September. Thousands of people always gather in the square to watch the ceremony and the Council's first thoughts were that the fly-past of Concorde could coincide with the time of the switch-on and that a radio message from the pilot to Danny asking him to 'pull the switch' at a given signal could be amplified and relayed to the waiting crowds. This proved to be technically very difficult, apart from the fact that it was realised that Concorde would be hardly seen in the dusk, and the idea was abandoned. Instead Concorde flew low over the Promenades and Tower in the afternoon of 8 September and Danny, who had been taken to the roof-top of a high multi-storey car park nearby, recorded a conversation with the pilot of Concorde. This was played back to the crowds later that evening as Danny was about to perform the actual Switch-On ceremony.

As the incredibly beautiful plane flew past it was low and seemed to be right over the Sun Lounge on the North Pier where popular Blackpool organist Raymond Wallbank interrupted his show to watch with his packed audience. Raymond told me that he had a special interest because he too was to take part in the Switch-On ceremony that evening.

Since early morning Town Hall officials and workmen had been putting the finishing touches to the months of hard work which go into each year's Illuminations Show at Blackpool. The stage for Danny and the Mayor's party had been erected in front of the Town Hall and a Hammond organ had been specially installed for the occasion.

It seems to be almost a traditional hazard at Switch-On ceremonies for at least some rain to fall, so precautions were taken for protecting the powerful loudspeakers and that day the lunch-time passers-by received something of a shock when Raymond Wallbank tested the equipment, and his lively signature tune, 'Who's Sorry Now?' boomed out across Talbot Square!

During the afternoon the final preparations to greet Danny and Toni Palmer, the leading lady from his shows, were completed. From 5 pm the crowd began to gather in Talbot Square. By 7.15 pm the Square was full and Danny and his party were having dinner with the Mayor at the Imperial Hotel.

At 7.30 pm Raymond Wallbank began his hour-long programme at the organ to entertain the crowds. 'Acknowledged as one of the most brilliant and versatile entertainers in Blackpool' (*The Stage*, 31 August 1972) Raymond Wallbank was naturally delighted to take part in the biggest civic event of the year. A quarter of a million people each year enjoy his two-hour musical show at the organ in the Sun Lounge on Blackpool's North Pier where for the last seven years his programmes of pop music, requests and sing-songs have made the Sun Lounge one of the happiest spots in Blackpool. By now people were hanging out of the windows and perched on rooftops.

Then it was almost time for Switch-On. Danny had the enormous crowd eating out of his hand. They simply loved it when he turned to Raymond and said 'Do you know the verse of

On Mother Kelly's Doorstep?' Raymond picked it out on the organ immediately and Danny had the crowd join in and sing along with him the tune that has become his signature tune.

At last it really was time to switch on the illuminations. Now, Raymond's Business Manager Lister Redman tells me that each visiting celebrity has a special surprise awaiting them when the switch is actually closed for the Lighting and Electrical Services Department always plans a pleasant and spectacular surprise for the guest of honour. This year was no exception. There was the roar of a cannon, a somewhat unexpectedly long pause, another explosion, a flutter of pigeons and then the whole front of the Town Hall burst into a blaze of light and a larger-than-life portrait of Danny appeared, to be followed by the rest of the illuminations along Blackpool's six-mile front.

After the switch-on Danny left the stage and went to the Mayor's Parlour. There he met Raymond Wallbank, who had been entertaining the crowd for so long, and Raymond's wife. Everyone present found Danny very relaxed and easy to get on with and he was certainly full of the magnificent reception the people had given him. Toni Palmer said how much they were both looking forward to coming to Blackpool. Advance bookings for the show, in fact, broke all records.

By now a steady drizzle had started but Raymond's lively music and happy personality soon had the huge crowd singing and laughing at his jokes although the rain made playing quite difficult and Raymond's fingers were literally splashing through the water on the keyboard!

Naturally, everyone was waiting to see Danny and a great roar went up as he appeared with the Mayor. Danny was immaculately dressed, as always, not in his stage costume of course but in an elegantly tailored brown velvet suit, set off by a cream shirt edged in brown. His tanned face and beaming smile brought a warm glow into the packed faces in front of him and he strode forward, cocked his thumb in the air and shouted: 'Wotcher mates!'

After the usual introductions and speeches Danny was presented with a huge stick of Blackpool rock, almost as big as himself, made specially by the Coronation Rock Company and Danny immediately announced that he was going to give it to charity. The recorded conversation with the Concorde pilot was played for the benefit of the crowd and then Danny left for his tour of the Lights, riding with the Mayor of Blackpool, Councillor Edmund E Wynne, and the Mayoress, the Hon Mrs Wynne, and other guests in an illuminated tramcar along the five-mile length of the promenade illuminations. As he sat in the coach outside the Town Hall, waiting for everyone else to get in, he wound down his window to talk to the crowd and by a strange coincidence the young girl he first spoke to was Raymond Wallbank's daughter, Linda. That personal touch certainly made one little girl's day; in fact the day was made for all those who were fortunate enough to meet Danny, it seems.

Danny was instantly recognised all along the route since he sat in an elevated position alongside the tram driver at the front of the cab and again he received rapturous welcomes from the crowds. The numbers that gathered in Talbot Square to see Danny perform the ceremony that 1972 evening were, Robert Battersby tells me, some of the largest ever recorded for this particular event and the police estimate of the crowd in Talbot Square and the adjoining street was ten thousand. Danny's welcome left no doubt as to how popular he is with a great section of the British public.

During the course of a speech at the Civic Dinner, given in honour of Danny that evening, the Mayor referred to the 1972 switch-on ceremony as the 'Danny and Connie Affair'; a reference which amused Danny no end.

On 14 September 1972, six days after the Blackpool Illuminations Switch-On, valuable paintings and antique furniture were damaged by fire at Danny's riverside home in Mill Lane, Henley (where his neighbour is Lady Peel, better known as actress Beatrice Lillie).

The luxury house, filled with antiques, had been purchased by Danny only a year before and had just been renovated and a swimming-pool added. The blaze (possibly electrical in origin) started in the basement and quickly spread to the living-room and the study, destroying carpets and furnishings. Danny was in London at the time and was unaware of the fire until it had been extinguished. Next day he went down to inspect the damage. His brother, Richard ('Dick'), who lives nearby at Goring, hurried meanwhile to the scene and said at the time: 'Danny will be brokenhearted when he sees what has happened.'

In the event there was no great damage to the structure of the house but many fittings and pictures were destroyed; and the cellar, stocked with rare and even priceless wines and drink, was badly affected. That nearly broke Danny's heart. He is a connoisseur of wine and had laid in a fine stock. In addition to that, when his London club had closed, he had had the excess drink transferred to Henley, and now much of it was ruined.

But Danny had received hard knocks before and his natural optimism and Roman Catholic faith helped him over another difficult patch; in addition he was rehearsing and opening a new show at Coventry, as Danny's Manager, Jack Hanson, mentioned to me in a letter at the time.

There is little doubt that Danny's Catholic upbringing is very important to any kind of understanding of the personality of the entertainer. He makes no secret of the fact that he is a practising Catholic and no one can argue about religion with Danny. He was, he says, talking to Cardinal Heenan on one occasion when Lord Longford said he would like to have him on his Commission on Pornography.

Danny was, as he puts it, 'a bit surprised'. 'I mean, I'm not a dirty performer. I'm naughty, like Max Miller in a frock. But when I had thought about it I had to tell him, sorry, but my image is all wrong for you, I'm much too cheeky. He wasn't put out. I don't know whether he likes my act but he did say he thought I did well what others do badly.' I don't know what Lord Longford thinks of Danny's act either; I can't think he would have approved of Danny's club act, but Lord Longford did tell me the circumstances of his invitation to Danny. He said, 'I was introduced to him at a Catholic function and was assured that he would make an excellent member of our Committee. Unfortunately he did not see his way to accept.' Lord Longford did not answer my request for his comments on Danny's refusal, or let me know his opinions and impressions of Danny as a man and as an entertainer. Neither did he elaborate on his approach to drag in general. I must say that I was surprised that Lord Longford issued such an invitation to Danny La Rue, a choice that could hardly have pleased Mary Whitehouse for Danny has repeatedly stated that he is against *any form* of censorship; one sentiment of his with which I find myself in complete agreement.

The Royal Command Performance at the London Palladium on 30 October 1972 raised over forty thousand pounds for the Variety Artiste's Benevolent Fund and Danny, a long-standing Member of the Grand Order of Water Rats, in his second Royal Variety Show presented *Salute the Stars* (musical director: Derek New) with David Ellen, the Tommy Shaw Dancers and The Derek New Singers; an act written by Bryan Blackburn.

Another artiste in this Royal Command Performance was Liberace, the American entertainer and singer, and a photograph of the two stars was reproduced on the front of *Private Eye*, dated 3 November 1972.

Danny looks upon Liberace as a good friend and when he stayed at The Swan they went round the village together. Liberace made purchases in most of the shops and everyone loved him.

During the course of his 'Command' performance Danny, resplendent as ever for his familiar and clever impersonations, became hilarious when, dressed in pink with giant pearls, he mocked the demure simper and insecure vowels of Twiggy.

Our Miss Fred, Danny's first film, released in December 1972, was set in France in the 1940s. Danny described his part as a sort of Charley's Aunt-cum-Scarlet Pimpernel and he wore fifteen different wigs and dyed his elegant silver hair for the first time ever. 'I'm more of a tart than I am on stage, more of a real bird,' he told Philip Oakes in October 1972, in an interview for the *Sunday Times*. 'In the theatre when someone tries to touch me up I put on a gruff voice and say, " 'Ere, watch it!". But in the film I have to stay really female.'

Danny played the part of Fred Wimbush, a British seaside entertainer, who is called up to join the army and sent to France. As soon as he reaches the army post he discovers that his reputation as a stage performer has preceded his arrival and he is already scheduled for duty in a camp show, portraying the heroine! The show goes along well until Fred, in full face and body make-up, wearing a wig and a stunning cocktail dress, makes his entrance only to find that the audience has vanished due to the arrival of some German troops.

There is no time for Fred to change and, hurriedly warned by his commanding officer not to disclose that he is a man or he will be shot as a spy, Fred acts out his disguise so convincingly that the enemy officer, General Brincker (Alfred Marks), with spine-chilling Teutonic chivalry, offers 'him' protection from the Gestapo.

At this point a diversion arrives in the shape of a small party of English girls from a finishing school, accompanied by their two harassed mistresses, Miss Fodden (Lally Bowers) and Miss Lockhart (Frances de la Tour) and coming across a female (as far as they are aware) in this battle area, they turn to Fred, who is now known as Frederika, for help and advice. Fred, much as he would like to, dare not reveal his true identity for he discovers that Miss Fodden is violently opposed to all men and accordingly her girls have been starved of male companionship for weeks.

An escape is planned with a view to reaching the French coast with the help of a battered old car which they christen Agatha. All this time Fred is becoming more and more anxious to get back into male attire and he suggests that during the escape he might be less noticeable dressed as a man; a plan that Miss Fodden considers doomed to failure.

Meanwhile the girls, unbeknown to their mistresses, have befriended and are hiding an RAF officer named Smallpiece (Lance Percival) whom they discovered trapped in a tree after a parachute descent. Smallpiece is immediately attracted by Frederika and receives a rude shock when Frederika not only produces name, rank and number but also asks for the loan of the officer's razor. Smallpiece then discloses a possible escape route to a secret airfield near Calais and with the help of Agatha it is decided to make the attempt.

Between whiles Fred's frustration knows no bounds as the girls, oblivious to his feelings, parade nonchalantly before him in their lingerie. Miss Lockhart, to make matters worse, has begun to idolise their sophisticated new friend.

Eventually, dressed as French peasants, they all board the old car and trundle across the enemy-infested countryside with Smallpiece stowed away in the boot among 'Frederika's' underwear. They succeed in avoiding the Germans and secure refuge in a hotel after Miss Fodden has more or less terrorised the proprietor and his wife into submission.

Fred, still on the look-out for fresh clothing, and none too particular about where he gets it, bursts into the bathroom of a top-brass German, Schmidt, who, through a cloud of steam, catches sight of an attractive female making off with his SS uniform. After a soapy skirmish, Schmidt, clad in nothing but a towel, dashes after the elusive Fred. He bumps into a girl wearing a frilly maid's outfit, pushes her aside and charges on; totally unaware that he has in fact encountered Fred who has made another quick change of costume.

Miss Fodden, by now more than a little disturbed by 'Frederika's' unladylike demeanour, is taken ill with suspected malaria and Fred, dressed for the event in belted trench coat and black beret, sets off after dark for a doctor.

As he reaches the doctor's house he is trapped in crossfire between German soldiers and two French Resistance fighters, one

of whom insists on swapping clothes with him. Fred finds himself
in front of his old adversary General Brincker, who decides that
'she' must never leave his sight. Next month, he insists, he will be
buying 'her' pretty dresses in London's Oxford Street.

Because Fred is now the General's lady, the girls persuade 'her'
to charm Brincker into giving them all leave passes and Fred,
quaking at what he must do, prepares to be wined and dined by
the General, accompanied by Smallpiece, in stolen SS uniform.
Unfortunately, or perhaps fortunately, the first person they see at
the local Palm Court is Schmidt so Fred promptly loses himself in
a crowd of Paris Mannequins, only to find that they are about to
give a fashion show. To his utter astonishment Schmidt finds
himself looking at 'Fred' in one dazzling ensemble after another
and Fred and Smallpiece manage to escape by the skin of their
teeth.

Brincker now tries to get 'Frederika' to help Dr Goebbels'
propaganda department and become a kind of Lady Haw-Haw,
enticing her countrymen to surrender but before the General can
exert pressure, Fred again tricks his way out of trouble.

With Brincker and Schmidt on the rampage, Fred and the girls
have no choice but to leave hurriedly and Agatha is again called
into action and splutters and explodes with German motor-cycle
troops giving chase as the party bluffs its way to Calais.

Reaching the airfield they face the obstacle of getting past the
sentries and decide that the only solution is for all of them,
including Smallpiece, Miss Fodden and Miss Lockhart, to pose as

'talent' from a nearby brothel on their way to liven up the German Barracks. Hilarious and outrageous activities bring the film to an appropriate close.

The many and sometimes puzzling twists in the plot provided Danny with material for plenty of comedy and impersonation but for many people the film just did not come off. I have talked with a number of people associated with *Our Miss Fred,* from Monty Berman whose firm 'dressed' the film (apart from Danny's costumes) to Miss Adrian McCarthy, a continuity girl and assistant to Bob Kellett who directed the film. She and others all agree that it was a very happy film while it was being made; there were lots of smiles and good humour.

The film was produced in colour and originally ran for ninety-six minutes but when it was given an AA Certificate, which meant that children under fourteen years of age could not see it, protests resulted in the Censor giving it an A Certificate (which meant that it could be seen by the whole family) provided two cuts were made. These concerned a song involving a bouncing ball and a short scene with Danny and others in a chase. Running time was thus reduced, in Britain, to ninety-four minutes.

Danny was, of course, tremendously popular during the making of the film. A perfectionist as always, he chose all his clothes, making sure of such details as the length of skirts in the 1940s and seams in stockings. Instead of resting between shots like other actors, he was always on the set, watching everything that was going on; to learn, as he put it, as much as he could. He enjoyed himself from start to finish – the five weeks in Norfolk and the five weeks in Hertfordshire – even if it did mean his having to get up very early each morning to be made-up by 7 am.

He spent about three hours each morning making himself up; it took that long to get into the part physically and mentally. And it was noticed that his voice was much better after lunch, seeming to improve as the hours of daylight passed. Not that he is alone in this respect, in fact he is in good company for Frank Sinatra always records after midday. On the other hand Danny was always wide awake and full of life at 11 pm and he never went to bed early. He pitches his voice much higher when he is in drag and he did seem more 'at home' in those parts of the film.

Considerable care was taken in casting the girls who played the parts of young English girls at finishing school (Kristin Hatfield, Seretta Wilson, Jenny Twigge, Vanessa Furse and Sophie Batchelor) and also the two mistresses, played in the end by Lally Bowers and Frances de la Tour. The great care that is always taken in selecting his supporting players has undoubtedly contributed to Danny's enormous success in the past. Danny's stand-in was a personal friend and he was the cause of a certain amount of good-humoured bantering during the making of the film, due to the fact that he stood about five feet in his socks and spent most of his time, as a stand-in, perched on top of a box! Danny also had with him Jimmy Hunt, who was to join the cast of Danny's show for the season at Blackpool; he acted as dresser and hairdresser and helped a lot with one thing and another. Jack

Above: Roy Hudd, Lionel Blair and Danny in high spirits during rehearsals for *Danny La Rue at the Palace*, 1970.

Below: Danny and the company in the fabulously successful *Danny La Rue at the Palace*, 1970.

Right: HRH Princess Margaret chats with Danny and other members of the cast backstage at the Palace Theatre, April 8, 1970.

Lower Right: Danny and Lord Snowdon enjoy a joke after the premiere of *Danny La Rue at the Palace,* held in aid of the Invalid Children's Aid Association, 1970.

Below: Danny as Fanny Oakley, with Roy Hudd in *Danny La Rue at the Palace,* 1970.

Left: Picking up some points on beauty. Danny with Miss World contestants at the Savoy Hotel, November 1970.

Right: The Variety Club of Great Britain's 1970 Annual Ladies' Luncheon at the Dorchester Hotel. Writer Mary Hayley Bell (right), actor John Mills (left) and a guest chat with Danny.

Left: Danny with a two-hundred-year old automatic drum-playing bear after he had opened the Kensington Antiques Fair, October 1971.

Above: Danny in SS uniform, enjoys a joke on the set of *Our Miss Fred* with fellow star Lance Percival.

Right: Our Miss Fred (1972) Danny's first film, was set in France in the 1940s and Danny wore fifteen different wigs and dyed his own hair for the first time ever for the part of Fred Wimbush who dons SS uniform in parts of the film.

Hanson turned up occasionally and was with the unit for about a week at one time in Norfolk. In Hertfordshire too he appeared sporadically, usually on business. When Danny considered buying a house in the county (he could hardly have gone wrong from a business point of view) Jack would view suitable properties and report back and then Danny would dash off and look over the places but nothing came of the idea.

The first five weeks' filming took place at Melton Hall, Melton Constable, seven miles from Fakenham in Norfolk. Here the unoccupied house and overgrown garden were cleverly transformed into something resembling occupied France in the 1940s; and here, in his spare time between shooting, Danny seemed to enjoy driving along the flat country lanes in his big Delarge with various youngsters as passengers. Driving such a car must have been quite a change from his tiny Triumph Stag which he used to get to and from the set.

While in Norfolk, Danny occupied the best room overlooking the sea at the Hotel de Paris, Cromer. The television film of his show at the Palace Theatre was screened during his stay there and he watched it avidly, with some invited members of the film unit, on the colour set in his room. He seemed to be very pleased with it.

Meticulous, as always, he invariably saw the rushes of the previous day's filming and, it was suggested to me, if he thought a hair was out of place, the scene was re-shot. It is ironic to think that this scrupulous attention to detail may, in the long run, have had an unfortunate effect on the finished production, for perfection itself can be destructive.

Sometimes, during the re-take of a re-take of a re-take, Adrian McCarthy would produce a 'Buck's Fizz' for Danny; a thoughtful gesture that pleased Danny who found the opportunity to repay her kindness. During the making of the film it happened to be Adrian's birthday and although, as far as she was aware, very few people knew, somehow Danny discovered and bought her a lovely travelling clock. This thoughtfulness is one of the most attractive facets of Danny's character and on completion of the film he gave individual and well-thought-out presents to everyone who had worked with him. Adrian McCarthy treasures a beautiful presentation decanter of champagne: a tangible reminder of a very happy association with a talented and, she feels, a very happy man.

During the filming Danny seemed to be very pleased with everything and everybody and would often take out for a meal various people working on the picture; one evening perhaps the camera-crew, another time the lighting technicians and so on. On one occasion Adrian McCarthy had dinner with Danny and about four other people. He took them to a small place at Holt – a farmhouse really – that supplied simple but excellent food and there Danny was interrupted several times during the meal, but he was never rude and always appeared to be only too delighted to sign his autograph or chat and joke for a minute with anyone. However, it is a different matter when he is called to the telephone. Then, wherever he is, he is very careful about whom he speaks to and only when the caller has satisfactorily identified himself will Danny come on the line.

On only about three occasions did the star of the film show any signs of temperament and each time, I was told, his attitude was more than justified. Although kindness itself most of the time, he is a very shrewd businessman, always aware of his image and alive to the potential of the end-product.

His good manners, immaculate clothes and general attractiveness during the filming, as elsewhere, helped to make him much-liked by the ladies and most of the men although he is not a man to suffer fools gladly.

The second half of the two-and-a-half months' filming was spent in Hertfordshire, two weeks at Panshanger, a private airfield near Hertford, and the remaining three weeks in the vicinity of Elstree. At this time Danny stayed at The Thatched Barn on the Barnet by-pass and it was there, about two weeks before the film was finished, that he gave a big party to about a hundred people who had worked on the film, a party that lasted all night and ended with dozens of people jumping into the swimming pool fully clad! The highlight of the meal was an enormous turkey in aspic with the word 'DANNY' picked out on it.

Among those present was Danny's sister Nancy, from Sussex. Danny always invited his mother to his parties but this time she had been very ill and Danny thought it best if she knew nothing about the event. When she did learn about it, she called him on the telephone and was livid!

At the film's *première* on 14 December Danny said, 'The film
was a great challenge to me but I think it's the best thing I have
ever done.' Not everyone agreed with him and Danny's
long-awaited film début didn't find favour with many of the
critics.

Felix Barker, in the London *Evening News* found that Danny
looked 'absolutely stunning in a red wig'; but he seemed to 'suffer
from no problems of coiffeur or costume; neither shot nor shell
blows a single hair out of place . . . and with hardly a blink of
apology the plot is twisted so that Danny can appear in a fashion
show (for the Germans) . . .' while Dilys Powell in the *Sunday
Times* was even less impressed. 'Everybody, I gather, idolises
Danny La Rue; I have seen him only in some fleeting television
appearances, and that hardly counts . . . I find I can live without
female impersonators,' she says before relating the somewhat
confused story (by Ted Willis with screenplay by Hugh Leonard)
ending her review by saying: '. . . a lot of expertise is spent on a
load of old British farce which culminates in a rude old British
song about the testicular deficiencies of the Nazi hierarchy. I never
thought to hear myself saying Come Back, Norman Wisdom.' Ian
Christie in the *Daily Express* headed his piece, 'Danny in drag
proves a miss' and David Robinson in the *Financial Times*
referred to the 'latest sacrifice of comic talent'. Fergus Cashin in
the *Sun* said, 'It should have been a slapstick scream but
unfortunately it's just a drag.' One staunch film devotee, a
knowledgeable and experienced film addict, told me: 'It is one of

the three worst films that I have ever seen; it really is excruciatingly bad.'

An extract from *Our Miss Fred* was shown on the London Weekend television chat-show, *Russell Harty Plus* on 19 December 1972, when something of Danny's great charm and personal magnetism came across and viewers were able to understand and accept as a simple statement of fact what Russell Harty said of Danny: 'Everyone who works with him, adores him.'

On 27 April 1973, BBC television transmitted a recording of *Stars of the Year*, Clubland's 'night of nights' from the stage of Batley Variety Club and Danny La Rue presented the Bernard Delfont Supreme Award to singer Barry Ward as the 'most promising newcomer of the year'. The show, *compèred* by David Nixon, consisted of club and television entertainers: Charlie Williams, Freddie Davies and The New Seekers and these stars entertained, introduced and presented *The Stage* awards to the five outstanding club acts of the previous twelve months, the stars of tomorrow. Before presenting the award to Barry Ward, Danny sang, straight and in male costume, *I Did it My Way*. During his stage shows he sometimes sings that song while in female dress and it was a measure of his calibre as an artist to have brought off such a number in this way, playing it against his usual act.

I asked David Nixon whether he would like to tell me about working with Danny but he said he couldn't really help because he had only appeared with Danny a couple of times. He added: 'I have a great regard for him . . . he is highly talented and one of the hardest working members of the entertainment profession.'

It is indisputable that much of the success enjoyed by Danny and other less famous but competent contemporary female impersonators, can be explained in terms of public demand and a new awareness. It was a case of doing the right kind of act at the right time. The enormous success of drag acts and female impersonation came about in the 1960s against a background of unrest and change in moral outlooks and standards.

It was a time when anything that had not previously been accepted, could and should be done, a time of broadening attitudes, of widening horizons, throughout entertainment generally and particularly in films and the theatre. It was a time for 'doing your own thing'; a time when *anything* was acceptable; a period of new thinking and enlightened audience participation. It was the perfect time for Danny to come into his own and he grasped every opportunity, kept one step ahead of the modern outlook and fashionable thinking and carved a niche for himself in the jungle of popular entertainment. John Fisher in his *Funny Way to be a Hero* (1973) suggests that if Danny's pre-eminence in the field of female impersonation proves anything, it probably proves that the general public is prepared to accept one, and only one, performer of his kind at any given time.

Danny's characterisations are, as we have seen, in the main lacquered and sharp-tongued career women of the present century. He has a great gift for catching the essential and underlying qualities of well-known figures and extending the impersonation almost to the point of caricature so that a recognised figure is presented with her female qualities and foibles exaggerated to outrageous and often hilarious proportions.

I have been interested in obtaining the opinions and convictions of many people in the realm of entertainment who feel that Danny's success lies to a great extent in his straightforward and clear-cut approach to the subject of 'female impersonation'; although this is an expression that Danny himself dislikes. He feels that the general public don't look upon him as a female impersonator but rather as a comic wearing dresses instead of a funny suit. 'Female impersonation', Danny finds, 'a tiny bit suspect.' He likes to think of himself as a comedian who dresses as a tart (his own way of describing himself on stage) while everyone 'out front' knows full well that there's a fellow underneath the sequins and the satins – 'that's the giggle'.

Veteran Music Hall star, George Wood ('Wee Georgie Wood') told me in May 1973, that he believes that Danny has been influenced by, more than anyone else, the great comedian Jimmy O'Dea (whose most famous character was 'Mrs Mulligan') and, rather more surprisingly perhaps, by Michael MacLiàmmóir; both, like Danny, Irishmen. It is an interesting speculation and something that could explain, in part at least, the marvellous *repartee* with his audience and the infallible and apparently effortless sense of timing and professionalism that pervades Danny's performances today.

I wrote to Michael MacLiammóir, asked him about Danny and

offered to go and talk with him in Dublin. He replied, in typical vein: 'Thank you so much for your letter. It is wonderful of you to suggest that you might come over to Ireland to see me . . . but I fear it would be a disappointing visit, although I would very much like to meet you again.

'The fact is I know so very little about Danny La Rue, except what everybody knows, that he is a phenomenon of unbelievable brilliance. That he is also, I am proud to say, a fellow townsman of mine and has still scores of relations there, while I have none, my family being from County Limerick and known to Cork only as the "Fly by Nights", for our residence there covered a mere eight years, is also factual, but of no vast interest especially as now I have told you all. Added to this, I only met Danny once. It was in London and my partner Hilton Edwards and I were entranced by an invitation from him to meet at the theatre where he was playing, and to dinner at his night club where we saw him give a ravishing performance. He was in every way a most charming host and invited us for the weekend to his house on the river. Most unhappily for us previous engagements prevented us from going. We regret it to this day. So, alas, the warmth of my admiration is only equalled by the scantness of my knowledge of him, and it is a matter of great regret. Perhaps Fate will be kinder in the future. But you see how little I have to tell you . . . I wish so much that I could be more revealing about the great Danny.'

The thing that Danny works hard at getting across is that he is not just 'a fellow impersonating a bird'; he is also a chap letting the birds know that he has caught on to them. They know that they are largely illusions created by hairdressing, make-up and dress sense – and in his act Danny makes sure that they know that he knows. It is an attitude that defines the effect of all the best female impersonation acts, carrying the presentation a stage further than mere impersonation. Danny has realised, as Roger Baker points out in his book *Drag*, that the male impersonator, even when the disguise is false and not intended to deceive, can touch a range forbidden to a man; a woman playing a man can sing songs that are sensitive and tender without causing embarrassment; a female impersonator must always be amusing. And Danny's patter, delivered with a brash directness almost worthy of Max Miller (a comparison Danny likes but he is not really comparable to the one and only Max), is so blue at times that it is unbelievable. His whole act is in fact a bewildering and quite unique combination of subtlety and the most obvious vulgarity; of topical comment and pure and unadulterated corn. What Danny really likes is innuendo, the *double entendre* but he gets by with his well-rehearsed repertoire and is honest enough to admit that his humour is broad.

He receives a lot of mail, mostly from older women but some from girls and children. He keeps lots of the drawings that children have sent him (although he says he's not superstitious) and he has quite a collection of dolls, little ones and big ones, that fans have given him. A few years ago some members of the fair sex, hearing of his liking for nougat, sent him six boxes then and have continued to send some ever since. It is a kind thought and Danny really values that kind of thoughtfulness. 'That sort of thing,' he says, 'the dolls, the letters and the nougat, all add up to one great big wonderful feeling of warmth.'

I went to see Monty Berman of Bermans and Nathans at 18 Irving Street, Leicester Square, the world's largest theatrical and film costumiers, the two famous businesses having been amalgamated in February 1972.

Bermans began as a Military Tailors in Leicester Square in 1900, where it was started by Morris and Max Berman, Monty's grandfather and father. In 1912 they moved to premises in Irving Street (then Green Street) and the shop has since become the head office and centre of the company that dressed Danny La Rue for eleven years – the first man they had ever seriously dressed as a woman – and they were delighted to dress him again for parts of the film *Our Miss Fred.*

The firm was badly bombed during the Second World War but afterwards, with Squadron Leader Monty Berman back from the Royal Air Force and into the business with his father and Fred Baker, Bermans soon became established as one of the leading television, theatrical and film costumiers.

Since then countless films, television productions and stage shows have been dressed by the House of Bermans. In the 1950s the stage presentation of *My Fair Lady* and the film *Moulin Rouge* are examples of the company's expertise, while in the 1960s Bermans dressed such diverse productions as *The Prime of Miss*

Jean Brodie, and *Oh! What a Lovely War,* in 1970, *Vivat! Vivat! Regina!, Cromwell, Patton* and *Ryan's Daughter;* and subsequently *Anne of the Thousand Days, Young Winston, Alice in Wonderland* and *Jesus Christ, Superstar.*

There is no doubt that Danny was very fortunate in having what is probably the finest and certainly the largest costuming business in the world to dress him in those all-important days when he was becoming successful.

Today the walls of the entrance hall at 18 Irving Street are covered with autographed photographs of entertainment personalities who have visited Bermans and Nathans and as Monty Berman told me, it is no exaggeration to say that nearly every personality in show business has at one time or another been fitted out at Bermans.

In recent years the company's business has extended to photographic sessions, publicity promotions, advertising commercials, costume exhibitions and of course colour television has increased the demand for their specialist knowledge. All this increased work has resulted in no less than six branches of Bermans in London (including a Ladies' Costume section which can produce with complete accuracy the most intricate period or high fashion garment to demanding deadlines which no fashion couture house in the world would normally handle), a branch on Santa Monica Boulevard in Hollywood (opened in 1949) and run by Monty's brother, David Berman; while later agencies were developed in Paris, Rome and Madrid.

It is not only the big film and television companies that bring business to Bermans for they cater also for fancy dress parties, bridesmaid's dresses and page boy's costumes; and many repertory companies and amateur dramatic societies and groups have costumes for their productions 'supplied by Bermans'. The company prides itself on giving the same high standard of attention to these enterprises as it maintains for professional productions.

As I talked with Monty Berman about Danny, it was obvious that here again was a man who valued the friendship and admired the talents and qualities of the 'king of drag'. At one point, I recall, I murmured with a smile that everyone seemed to say the same wonderful things about Danny: 'he seemed almost too good to be true!' 'But he is!' said Monty. 'He's a wonderful man. For example, he always goes out of his way to ensure that the work done for him is appreciated. After dressing *Our Miss Fred* (apart from Danny's costumes) Danny made a point of seeking me out and telling me, "Monty, your boys have done a marvellous job – as usual." ' This, Monty Berman told me, he thought was the mark of a real professional.

Monty Berman says he loves Danny's act but even if you don't happen to like the female impersonation bit, you could not help but like the tremendous personality of the man. When Danny's club had been established about two years he decided to form an association that would be responsible for all his dresses and Monty told me that he has always maintained that the personal letter

Danny wrote to him at the end of their business association was one of the most charming letters that he had ever received. It was full of regret that circumstances made it necessary to leave the 'House of Bermans' and laden with gratitude and appreciation for the wonderful help and assistance he had received over the years. Monty told me, as he told Danny, that he quite understood; and today Monty has nothing but the kindest thoughts for Danny or, as he put it: he wishes Danny everything that is good for he is a true professional and a delightful man.

The Revue Department of Bermans looks after the hire costume side of the business and has been responsible for dressing many spectacular London Palladium productions and West End musicals. There, in Rupert Street, the Manager of the Ladies Dress Section is Peter MacAndrew and, since he and his staff had conducted day to day business with Danny, Monty Berman was good enough to arrange for me to visit that department of the establishment.

Peter MacAndrew told me that Danny, during the middle 1950s and early 1960s, would call monthly to arrange for either stock or new outfits for himself. The firm normally made six outfits at a time, which adds up to a lot of dresses!

Danny, I learned, had first come to Bermans when they were in Orange Street and he appeared unforgettably dressed: looking like a 'natty city gent'; he saw Cynthia Tingley on that occasion and she later, on behalf of Bermans, designed some of Danny's fabulous gowns.

Danny would usually come for three fittings in those days and a representative from Bermans would attend one rehearsal of a new show, usually on the Sunday before it opened. Peter MacAndrew related to me one of his most vivid memories of these Sunday rehearsals. This one was at Winstons Club where Danny and Maggie Fitzgibbon appeared in a mermaid sequence, their feet encased in the tails with long zip fasteners up the front of the costumes. Danny's zip had stuck and Peter, using the well-known trade dodge of rubbing the zip with the lead of a pencil, began to release the zip but Danny was almost late for his appearance (an unheard of event) and Peter remembers with a smile Danny's tiny feet encased in this mermaid's tail, flip-flip-flipping in tiny hops up the many steps from his dressing-room, with the rest of Danny's larger body weaving about as he maintained his balance!

At Bermans in Rupert Street I also met Miss Doris Gardiner who had made some of Danny's dresses and together they recalled a flesh-coloured leotard with sequins; a very sexy Nell Gwynne costume; a magnificent purple, gold and black creation for an Elizabeth I number; the ballet costumes for the Fonteyn and Nureyev number (Ronnie Corbett taking the part of Nureyev); the Lady Docker extravaganza and many more.

Doris told me that Danny always had really good ideas for his clothes: 'he has a far better idea of fashion and what suits him than many women.' 'So perfect were some of his characterisations and impersonations,' Peter added, 'that it was honestly difficult to believe that Danny and his female impersonation were the same person and very often people behind the scenes have asked, quite seriously, where the woman has gone, when Danny has re-appeared in male attire.'

I asked Peter whether Danny ever showed signs of being temperamental during his visits to Bermans as I know that this facet of an entertainer's personality was often encountered by his dresser and those responsible for his costumes. Peter said that Danny showed practically no temperament at all and on the few occasions when he was put out, he was justified in being annoyed and absolutely right in his estimation of the remedy.

I left Bermans with Doris Gardiner's final remark, so typical and yet so sincere: 'He is such a nice person and so kind, always remembering people who helped him, no matter how slightly.'

I also visited Daniel Farson, author, television interviewer and scriptwriter, at his lovely coastal home in North Devon. He regaled me with stories of Danny whom he had known, and photographed, when Danny had a flat near Regents Park's Zoo (later he took a flat not far from Charing Cross Road) and they had lunched together at Kettner's in Soho, where Daniel Farson was somewhat surprised at the treatment Danny La Rue received from the staff; waiters approaching the table, congratulating him on his success and saying how honoured they were to see him again. Danny, with a generosity of mind as well as of pocket that is rare in show business, invariably recalled immediately the person he was addressing and asked all the right questions, frequently mentioning the man's family, much to the waiter's gratification.

Daniel Farson, who became well known on television for his regular appearances on *This Week,* interviewing such personalities as Harold Macmillan, Colin Wilson and Caitlin Thomas, later produced a much researched book on *Marie Lloyd and Music Hall* and a fascinating work on *Jack the Ripper* (another subject he had dealt with on television). He first met Danny at a cocktail party at the old Winstons Club in the early 1960s.

Danny had seen a television programme Daniel Farson had made on old-time music hall that included that grand old singer Ida Barr (1882-1967) and during the course of conversation Danny remarked on her splendid appearance, adding, 'I'm so glad she's one of the few who were able to save some money.' Sadly, this was far from true and Daniel Farson explained that in fact Ida Barr existed on national assistance and lived in a drab tenement block that looked more like a prison than anything else behind Charing Cross Road.

Ida Barr was 'stage mad' for as long as she could remember and at fifteen she ran away to Ireland to join the chorus of a pantomime. She was good and the public liked her and she played in the London production of *The Sultan of Morocco* before running off again, this time to America, where before long she saw her name in lights in Los Angeles. When she returned to England she brought with her a new dance craze, ragtime, and a song that helped to make her famous, *Everybody's Doing it.* The other song forever associated with the red-haired girl they billed as 'Naughty but Nice' is the one she made her signature tune, which she always sang with sincerity, as a love-song: *Oh! You Beautiful Doll!*

Daniel Farson made the television film of old-time music hall stars (a programme that was entered as the ITV choice in the Montreux Festival) and inevitably Ida Barr gave a fabulous performance.

Some days later Danny telephoned Daniel Farson to say that he had arranged a surprise Benefit Show for Ida Barr (he arranged one for Jimmy James too) and would Daniel Farson arrange for her to come to a club in Brixton. Daniel Farson recounts what happened in his book, *Marie Lloyd and Music Hall:*

> When we arrived Ida was greeted by a crowd of film stars and aristocratic villains; Danny La Rue and his friends gave a complete Music Hall Show. As this was meant as a surprise I hadn't told her about the Benefit and this was a mistake – she was mystified, and confused, too overwhelmed to sing one of her old numbers in spite of cries of encouragement. When the owner of the club presented her with a cheque, she stuffed it straight into the caverns of her handbag which put a slight damper on the climax of the evening. Later, I saw her take the cheque out surreptitiously and she burst into tears when she realised the Benefit had given her eight hundred pounds. It was characteristic of Danny La Rue that he kept in the background and received less recognition than anyone, though this was entirely his own idea and must have cost him a lot in time and trouble. For Ida eight hundred pounds was a fortune. It enabled her to buy the luxuries that can make such a difference to life – at any age.

During their lunch together Danny La Rue told Daniel Farson,

'My act is the hardest to get away with in the profession. Let's face it, it *was* frowned on, and it can't work if it's offensive.'

Daniel Farson feels that Danny's great achievement is not that he has made female impersonation accepted, but rather that he has made it fashionable. 'Danny walks the tightrope of glamour with the safety-net of sending himself up at the same time,' he told me. 'He disarms the audience within a few seconds and the wives (laughing just a little too loudly) as well as their husbands, the toughs (careful not to laugh too loudly) and the others are not quite sure what to do.'

And then came the inevitable reference to the sudden booming voice of a brawny workman: 'Wotcher, mates!' emitted from the 'stately' and gilded façade of the 'feller dressed up as a tart', Daniel Farson used the word 'stately' because he found something formidable in Danny's appearance. 'He might send himself up, but God help the person who tries to send him up!' Hecklers, in fact, are swiftly disposed of. 'The drunken ones just make a noise,' Danny said. 'The others are seasoned, like performers, but they can't win, the lights are on *me!*'

Seated comfortably at a low table, near a window overlooking a delightful Devon bay and the restless sea as background music, I heard much from Dan Farson about the 'alert and handsome, grey-haired man who regards "professionalism" as a code to live by.' Danny, I was reminded, was totally reliable in his work; he leaves nothing to chance and there was a phrase that had stuck in Daniel Farson's mind; Danny had said, revealingly, 'Work is my alcohol.'

Indeed, his capacity for work is almost unbelievable. It was by no means unusual for him to appear in cabaret, beginning at 1.30 a.m., after an evening in pantomime, with rehearsals for another show, a television, radio, or press interview and some charity or personal appearance all fitted into twenty-four hours. When he began the run of *Danny La Rue at the Palace* and was still appearing at his own night club, his manager Jack Hanson predicted that 'everyone else may fall by the wayside but if Dan can crawl on, he'll do it.'

When he was on tour and still had his club Danny was lucky to get four hours' sleep a night, but then he regards sleep as a waste of time. The moment the curtain was down he would dash to his car to be driven to the club; and once, when he was delayed by fog on the road from Coventry, he didn't arrive until 1.30 am and was nearly a nervous wreck with worry that he wouldn't get there in time. He hates travelling in make-up but on occasions has no option so then he just removes the lipstick, puts on dark glasses, and prays that there won't be an accident!

Danny has only really missed one show in his whole career. Once he had a nasty fall during a performance and afterwards, when he was in agony, his doctor told him not to go on but he ignored the advice and, oddly enough, as soon as he was on stage, the pain disappeared.

He has always been generous in his dealings with other entertainers and often helps people in the industry when he can.

Drag star Ricky René can be said to have captivated Europe with his clever and beautifully dressed portrayals of the *femme fatale,* with Marlene Deitrich and Mae West among his most successful impersonations. In the business since 1955, René designs all his own costumes and, like Danny, the bulk of his fan mail comes from ladies. He enjoys the Lancashire audiences and now has a house at Southport.

When the American star opened his own club the press were quick to whip up stories of bitter rivalry between the two artistes. But when Daniel Farson went to the opening night party, who should arrive at the same time but Danny La Rue. He went straight up to René and wished him every success. Everyone thought this was 'pretty big' of Danny but he is very sincere in his admiration and kind thoughts towards other artistes. In a few months Ricky René's club had closed.

Once, when Avis Bunnage fell ill, Joan Littlewood asked Danny to take over her part for the night in the show, *Oh! What a Lovely War.* So well did Danny use his talents to portray someone else without projecting himself that most of the audience were unaware of the substitution.

Few female impersonators have received such publicity as Danny but by now everyone knows that anything he does will be well done, with that special 'professionalism' that he is so justly proud of. Even when he plays an ugly sister in pantomime, his gowns are stunning, but, as Danny says: 'You don't need to be ugly to be hated. Where does viciousness begin, but from an ugly nature? I play the part as a vicious, hard bird who isn't going to let the younger, prettier and inexperienced sister get away with it. But of course the kids know what it's all about. I've never known such participation; I used to shadow-box with them and they'd make faces at me . . . '

His striving for 'professionalism' extends to the whole of the cast in his shows and he has been brilliant in choosing exactly the right supporting actors and actresses for his talents: people like Victor Spinetti, Barbara Windsor, Ronnie Corbett, Maggie Fitzgibbon, Roy Hudd, Richard Wattis and Alan Haynes. And he always tries to give encouragement to the artistes appearing in his shows. He feels that there are too many people waiting to find fault; encouragement is so much more constructive. Tolerance too he considers to be important as intolerance leads to misunderstanding. All too often one hears such expressions as 'dreadful . . . disgraceful . . . inexcusable . . . ' but these remarks are made by people who rarely try to find out the whys and the wherefores.

Danny's Summer Season at the Opera House, Blackpool in 1973, the *Danny La Rue International Spectacular* (in effect it was very similar to *Danny La Rue at the Palace*) was no exception regarding the choosing of talented supporting players and to such tested and tried associates as David Ellen and Toni Palmer, Danny added Mike Goddard, a very clever comic; Jenny Layland, a beautiful and vivacious dancer; and Jimmy Hunt, a singer.

During the show Danny, appearing in female costume

throughout, had eleven changes varying from Cleopatra to Ginger
Rogers; the impersonations apart from Ginger Rogers, included
Mae West and Dorothy Squires and were very well done,
although I thought I glimpsed a certain sadness in Danny's whole
performance, almost as though the fact that he would be more
than happy to finish with dressing-up as a woman was beginning
to show; but overall it was a beautifully-staged, well-timed,
buoyant, musical and colourful show with the Tommy Shaw
Dancers and the Derek New Singers in fine form especially in a
hunting scene, *Riding High.* I learned afterwards that there was
some bitchiness and petty squabbling backstage and that more
than one person in the show was glad when it ended; but as
much can be said of practically any show.

It was interesting to hear Danny mention Larry Grayson's
famous characters, 'Slack Alice' and 'Everard' (as Larry refers to La
Rue characters in his act) and if some of the humour jarred, as
when Danny said 'God forgive me' and crossed himself, or the
corny one about his measurements came out again; on the whole
the show seemed to be thoroughly enjoyed by the predominantly
middle-aged audience. More than one person said to me afterwards
that it was not a man's show; so perhaps I may be forgiven for
not enjoying it as much as I had hoped. It was a lavish
production; no expense had been spared to make it really
spectacular. The front cloth alone, with 'Danny La Rue' in
coloured lights (later used at the Prince of Wales show in
London) cost two thousand four hundred pounds. 'But that's only

a fraction of the total cost,' Danny told Dennis Holman of *New Reveille* in November 1973. 'All the way through the audience gets the best that money can buy.'

It was typical of Danny, accompanied by his mother, to entertain, at the end of September 1973, the theatre box-office staff to a dinner at Blackpool's Green Dolphin restaurant; a happy affair that lasted until almost 3 am when Danny chartered a fleet of taxis to transport his guests safely home.

While in the show Danny rented a house in Hornsey Road and he was often to be seen at a local hotel, dining with a few friends. In general, he liked to keep away from the public and take things as quietly as possible. The last time he had played Blackpool was a season at the old Queen's Theatre where he was paid £6.50 a week! This time Danny appeared in full colour on the front of a Special Summer Number of *The Stage* (16 August, 1973) and Bernard Delfont described him, in an introductory article, as 'the club act supreme'. Referring to Danny's West End club Delfont went on to say, revealingly, that many cabaret graduates are still most enjoyed when they revert to intimate cabaret performances. Here, perhaps, lies Danny's future as an entertainer.

In September 1973, Danny was Guest Star in one of the 'Young Generation Big Top' television shows from Pontings Holiday Camp at Blackpool. Putting aside his wigs and falsies for the night, he opened the show by singing *Those Good Old, Bad Old Days*. After a few saucy jokes he introduced other turns which included Sandie Shaw, Trevor Chance and, from his own

Blackpool show, Mike Goddard. Danny appeared in three changes of male costume and sang, with five young children *Old MacDonald Had a Farm* and, with Sandie Shaw, the inevitable *On Mother Kelly's Doorstep.* Everyone I spoke to afterwards felt that Danny was better in drag.

It is likely that Danny's invariable practice of ending his club act by appearing in male attire was a final reminder that sent his audience home happy and contented that he was merely playing a part for them; and this idea does more than anything else to round off his superb impersonations and beautifully-dressed female characterisations. This final appearance is in great contrast to the booming voice and growling asides occurring in his acts and always receives a warm response. Gone are all traces of paint and powder, feathers, frills and wigs and onto the stage bounds a handsome and debonair Irishman, with twinkling eyes and saucy smile; the successful and accomplished entertainer *par excellence:* the man who is a myth in his own time.

And it looked as though the myth would become a memory when in November 1973, Danny announced that his new London show, opening at the Prince of Wales theatre the following month, would be his last show completely in drag.

'Frankly,' he said at the time. 'I don't want to go on dressing like a tart all my life.' He added, according to the *Daily Mirror* of 20 November, 'I know I've shattered box offices all over England but I think I've given back what I owed to the theatre and I just don't want to do it any more.'

'I plan to just be myself,' he went on. 'I hope to do plays – not Shakespeare – and present acts.' Roderick Gilchrist in the *Daily Mail* quoted Danny as saying just before the show opened: 'I am now forty-six. I've been fabulously successful and had tremendous fun but I think the time has come to change direction. I know I can't get any better so rather than go downhill from here I have decided to say goodbye to Lady Cynthia Grope and all the other dollies I play. So many colleagues in show business have overstayed their welcome and there has to come a time when a performer says "This is it." In future I want to appear in straight acting or comedy; perhaps a Feydeau farce or a Restoration comedy, playing the fop. I know it means a drop in money. I'm quite prepared for that. I don't even care if I'm not top of the bill.' With earnings estimated at over a hundred and fifty thousand pounds a year that have almost made him a millionaire, Danny had this to say of his career so far: 'I admit to being bawdy but I am totally unashamed of anything I have ever said or done. I'm not a dirty performer. Anybody can get a laugh by coming on and dropping their drawers but I make glamorous-looking ladies funny.' And, businessman to the end, he added, 'I believe this show will be the best I've done.'

Actually it was a good show but then it did cost well over a hundred and fifty thousand pounds to stage. A gala *première* for charity was held on 17 December with the proceeds going to SOS, the Stars Organisation for Spastics, and the Variety Club of Great Britain which helps sick, orphaned, handicapped and deprived children anywhere in the United Kingdom, regardless of race, colour or religion.

On the stage at the *première* Danny was presented with a cigarette box with a Gold Heart suitably inscribed and at a party afterwards he was presented with a portrait of himself by SOS. The party was held at the home of Princess Alexandra the Honourable Mrs James Ogilvy and those present included Diana Dors and Leslie Crowther.

A few days later Danny was named 'Rat of the Year' by the Grand Order of Water Rats in recognition of his work for charity. Lord Snowdon was guest of honour at the Rats' Ball, held at Grosvenor House, when Danny won the recognition *in absentia* and Vera Lynn was voted Show Business Personality of the Year.

Danny's third West End Show was presented by Bernard Delfont and Richard M Mills, it was directed by Freddie Carpenter, and the choreography was by Tommy Shaw. The writer was Bryan Blackburn, the designs by Berkeley Sutcliffe, the lighting by Michael Northen, and Mark Canter designed a completely new wardrobe (executed by Isolyn). The Tommy Shaw Dancers, the Derek New Singers and the orchestra conducted by Derek New, all took part.

Tommy Shaw trained with the Celtic Ballet and Ballet Jooss, he danced in a number of West End shows, staged dances in revue and pantomime and choreographed Danny's shows in Coventry, Manchester and Blackpool.

Berkeley Sutcliffe, who designed the ornamental clock at

Fortnum and Mason, has been connected with such shows as Hermione Gingold's revue *Rise Above It, Finian's Rainbow,* Jack Hulbert and Cicely Courtneidge comedies and classic productions, including Shakespeare, at the Old Vic Theatre.

Michael Northern trained with Jack de Leon at the old 'Q' Theatre, became associated with the Royal Opera House where he has been responsible for lighting many productions including *Ondine* for the Royal Ballet. Musical shows on which he has worked include *Charlie Girl, Canterbury Tales, The Val Doonican Show* and the later Danny La Rue shows.

Supporting Danny were talented Mike Goddard; song and dance comedian David Ellen; comedienne Clovissa Newcombe (who worked with Danny at his Hanover Square club); dancer Jenny Layland, who was with Danny at Manchester in *Queen of Hearts* and, more recently, in his Blackpool show; singer Jimmy Hunt, another veteran of Danny's club and the Blackpool show. The cast also included the clever young magician Johnny Hart, fresh from successful appearances at Las Vegas, Beirut and the *Ed Sullivan Show* in America; but apart from Danny himself the hit of the show was the act of the fabulous Los Diablos Del Bombo who were also in the Blackpool show with Danny. Their sensational speciality act of dance, drums, swords and *boleadoras,* performed with breathtaking speed, precision and zest has deservedly won them successful engagements in the Americas, Belgium, Greece and Paris, culminating with the Royal Variety Performance at the Palladium in 1972. In only a few years these

July 1970. Danny becomes the owner of The Swan Inn, Streatley and realizes two ambitions: to operate a good country hotel and to own an island.

five Argentinians, after training solidly for four months, perfected a unique and exciting act and it is another example of Danny's talent for picking winning acts to recall that the Los Diablos Del Bombo appeared in their first British show with Danny at Coventry Theatre.

In some respects the Prince of Wales show was the mixture as before: the one joke throughout could be described as phallic *double entendre;* but if there was little originality, it sparkled with enthusiasm and professionalism and Danny worked hard to good effect as Cleopatra, Nell Gwynne, Mother Bunny, Mae West, Carol Channing, Zsa Zsa Gabor, Liz Taylor and even Princess Anne. Altogether it was a most enjoyable show and a fitting end to Danny's career as a drag artiste, if that career is ended.

Looking back in 1973 on a career studded with success Danny admitted that he couldn't say that he was all that ambitious any longer. 'I've got a marvellous home and great friends. Nothing I do now could give me more than I have now.'

Of course it hadn't been as easy as it may seem in retrospect. Danny has always worked tremendously hard, far harder than most people realise. He knew, better than anyone, that his shows depended on his presence, his audience-pulling power, his high standard of performance and his example to the rest of the cast. Without him there would be no show and therefore he always worked just that much harder to ensure, as far as he possibly could, the success of the show and in so doing, the employment and the livelihood of everyone connected with the undertaking.

Just occasionally Danny allows himself to think back to the hard times, as he did once with Shirley Bassey who has also known dark days; and in the end they both agreed that they didn't regret any of those years, not even the really tough ones. It had all been worth while. Those times as much as the good and successful spells have helped to make Danny what he is today, a self-confessed contented man: 'I love my audience and my fans. I love my work. I'm happy. That's more than enough to be going on with.'

Acknowledgements

THE AUTHOR GRATEFULLY ACKNOWLEDGES HIS INDEBTEDNESS TO:

Robert Battersby, Raymond Wallbank and Lister Redman for information concerning Danny La Rue's switching on the lights at Blackpool

Gladys and Violet Bennett for talking about Danny La Rue and imparting something of their love for London and its theatres

Alec Berg for his memories of days gone by

Monty Berman for sparing time to talk and for putting him in touch with Peter MacAndrew and Doris Gardiner who knew and worked with Danny La Rue

Mrs Esmé Cooper and Mrs Pauline Simond for their help in presenting a picture of Danny La Rue in his early acting days

Crispin Derby for his continual encouragement, wise counsel, extensive practical assistance and many helpful suggestions

Pamela Derby for her valued help, advice and encouragement

Daniel Farson for his hospitality and generous help

Maggie Fitzgibbon for finding time to help when she was busy rehearsing a new play

Cyril Fletcher for his interest and helpful advice

Ted Gatty for some of his memories

Sir Alec Guinness for his helpful comments

Larry Grayson who helped enormously – in spite of his bad back (!)

Jack Hanson, Danny La Rue's manager, for his courtesy and help

Benny Hill for so politely pointing out that he is not a drag artiste

Rex Jameson ('Mrs Shufflewick') for an introduction to Old Time Music Hall and for all his help

Lord Longford for his help

Mrs Agnes Lukan, Mrs Honor Ratcliffe, Mrs Peggy Reeves, John R Waldron and all the other people who remember Danny Carroll when he was a youngster in Devon

Adrian McCarthy for providing a behind-the-scenes view of the film *Our Miss Fred* and to John and Pauline Thompson for making this meeting possible

Michael MacLiàmmóir for permission to quote from his letter

Alan Melville who put me on the track of information

John Mills, Wendy Craig (and her husband Jack Bentley) and all the other show business people for their kindness and assistance.

'Mister Smith' and the other drag artistes who were so kind and helpful

David Nixon for his help

Philip Oakes for his interesting observations

Ralph Reader for information about early drag entertainment

Gerry Slinger of Blighty's Club for revealing a treasured memory of Danny La Rue

Victor Spinetti for talking to me about Danny

The staff of The Swan Inn, Streatley, for making my visit so enjoyable

Mary Talbot for telling me the story behind her portrait of Danny

Chris Underwood for his interest and thoughtful help in many ways

Carla Wansey-Jackson for details about her meeting with Danny La Rue

Richard Wattis for his kindness and helpful letter

Lord 'Ted' Willis who couldn't have been more helpful

George ('Wee Georgie') Wood who went to a lot of trouble on my behalf

To my wife Joyce, who has travelled hundreds of miles with me in search of drag, and has helped more than she can ever know by just listening

To the personnel of the YWCA, YMCA, The Admiralty, Ministry of Defence, The Patent Office, The Board of Trade, The Registry of Business Names, BBC, Northcott Theatre Exeter, Churchills Night Club, British Film Institute, Cork City Corporation and the Society of Authors for valuable specialist knowledge and unfailing courtesy

To Vincent Firth of *Film Review*, Alix Coleman and Peter Genower of *TV Times*; Dennis Holman of *New Reveille*; Peter Tipthorp of *Annabel*; Sydney Edwards of the London *Evening Standard*; Roderick Gilchrist of *Daily Mail*; Russell Miller of *Daily Mirror*; Laurence Dobie of the *Guardian*; Philip Oakes of *Sunday Times* and their respective editors for permission to quote from articles in these periodicals. And to the following who have assisted with photographs: Mrs Esmé Cooper, Rex Jameson, Larry Grayson, Daniel Farson, Mrs Agnes Lukan, John R. Waldron, Central Press Photos Ltd, Syndication International, Associated

Press Ltd, David Steen and Camera Press Ltd, Tom Hustler and Keystone.
The author has made every effort to trace and acknowledge copyright material included in this book; should there be any omission in this respect he and his publishers apologise and undertake to make appropriate acknowledgement in future editions.

Select Bibliography

Baker, Roger   *Drag*   1968

Costa, Mario A   *Reverse Sex*   1962

Farson, Daniel   *Marie Lloyd and Music Hall*   1972

Fisher, John   *Funny Way to be a Hero*   1973

Hirschfeld, Hagnus   *Sexual Anomalies and Perversions*   (no date)

Marlowe, Kenneth   *Mr Madam: Confessions of a Male Madam*   1965

Montmorency, Desmond   *The Drag Scene*   1970

Newton, Esther   *Mother Camp: Female Impersonators in America*   1972

Underwood, Peter   *Horror Man – the Life of Boris Karloff*   1972

Index

ALEXANDRA, PRINCESS, 175
Alice in Wonderland, 160
Aladdin, 41
America, 21, 118, 165, 176
An Actor's Revenge, 128
An Evening with Danny La Rue, 91
Andrews, Julie, 91
Annabel magazine, 117
Anne, HRH Princess, 178
Anne of the Thousand Days, 160
Apollo Theatre, London, 46
April Folly, 68, 69
Arnold, Tom, 76, 86
As You Like It, 128
Aunt Edwina, 130
Australia, 105

BABES IN THE WOOD, 82
Babette, 98-99
Bagatelle Club, 74
Bailey, Pearl, 21
Baker, Fred, 159
Baker, Roger, 158
Baker, Stanley, 121
Ballet Jooss, 175
Barker, Felix, 153
Barnes, Clive, 60
Barr, Ida, 165-166
Barrie, Sir James, 131
Bart, Lionel, 105
Bassey, Shirley, 179
Batchelor, Sophie, 145
Batley Variety Club, 154
Battersby, Robert S., 131, 132, 137
Baxter, Stanley, 22
Beatles, The, 37, 85
Beaumont, Roma, 34
Beirut, Lebanon, 176
Belgium, 176
Bell, Mary Hayley, 45
Benjamin, Louis, 47
Bennett, Violet and Gladys, 32-39
Bentine, Michael, 104
Bentley, Jack, 45
Berg, Alec, 11-12, 13
Beringer, Esmé, 128
Berkshire, 112, 116, 117, 125, 137
Berman, David, 160
Berman, Monty, 144, 159-162
Bermans and Nathans, 32, 38, 159-164
Bernhardt, Sarah, 103, 128
Birds of a Feather, 42
Birthday Show, The 1969, 93, 101
Black and White, The, 68
Blackburn, Bryan, 105, 139, 175
Blackpool, Lancs, 23, 93, 131-137, 170-171, 172, 173, 175, 176
Blair, Lionel, 105
Blighty's Club, Farnworth, 23, 47

Blitz, 105
Bloomsbury, London, 66
Bond Street, London, 77, 80
Borocourt Hospital, Wyfold, Berks, 125
Bowers, Lally, 141-145
Bradfield, Berks, 125
Brighton, Sussex, 40
Bristol, Somerset, 71, 74
British Aircraft Corporation, 132
British Broadcasting Corporation, 123, 154
Brixton, London, 166
Broadway, New York, 107, 118
Broodway, Van de Clyde, 98-99
Bryan, Dora, 34
Bryden, Ronald, 103
Bunnage, Avis, 169
Business Names Act, 28
Butlin's Holiday Camps, 104
Bygraves, Max, 105
Byng, Douglas, 80

CAESAR, JULIUS, 82
Call It a Day, 67, 69
Cambridge Circus, London, 70, 103
Can-Can, 105
Canter, Mark, 88, 175
Canterbury Tales, 176
Cargill, Patrick, 129
Carpenter, Freddie, 105, 175
Carroll, Daniel (Danny La Rue), birth, 50; childhood, 51; youth, 51-52; scouting, 52; religion, 51, 122; first work, 53; Royal Navy, 58-59; first parts, 59; early drag shows, 70-71; stage name, 73; becomes a star, 80; Hanover Square Night Club, *q.v.;* wigs, 112-113; buys Swan Inn, 116; own best critic, 121; philosophy, 179
Carroll, Mrs Mary Ann, 43, 50, 51, 58, 66, 152
Carroll, Nancy, 51, 58, 66, 152
Carroll, Richard ('Dick), 50, 137
Carroll, Thomas, 50
Carte, Richard D'Oyly, 103
Carter, Lynne, 21
Cashin, Fergus, 153
Champion, Harry, 34
Chance, Trevor, 172
Channing, Carol, 178
Chaplin, Charles, 10, 18
Charing Cross Road, London, 164, 165
Charisse, Cyd, 105
Charley's Aunt, 46, 102, 104, 129
Charlie Girl, 105, 176
Chevalier, Maurice, 129
Ch'ien Lung, 128
China, 60-61, 128
Christie, Ian, 153
Churchills Club, 35, 36, 37, 73, 74, 77, 80, 81, 86
Cinderella, 59
Clacton-on-Sea, Essex, 104

Cleopatra, 171, 178
Coburn, Charles. 124
Cockran, Charles B., 103
Coleman, Alix, 118
Coliseum Theatre, London, 104
Collins, Sheila, 69
Come Spy With Me, 39-40, 89, 90
Commission on Pornography, 138-139
Companies Act, 28
Concorde 002, 132, 133, 136
Congreve, William, 130
Contemporary Films, 128
Cooper, Mrs Esmé, 69-70
Cooper, Henry, 18
Cooper, Tommy, 105
Corbett, Ronnie, 37, 81-82, 163, 170
Cork, Ireland, 50, 157
Coronation Rock Company, 136
Coronation Street, 77
Courtenay, Tom, 46
Courtneidge, Cicely, 33, 104, 176
Coventry, Warwick, 93, 101, 138, 168, 175, 178
Coward, Noel, 18
Cowardy Custard, 105
Craig, Wendy, 45
Cromwell, 160
Crosby, Bing, 10
Crowther, Leslie, 175
Cryer, Barry, 28, 105
Cushman, Robert, 10

DAILY EXPRESS, 153
Daily Mail, 174
Daily Mirror, 173
Daily Mirror Magazine, 72
Dale, Philip, 46
Dancing Years, The, 34
Danny La Rue at The Palace, 89, 93, 102-106, 108, 120-121, 150, 168, 170
Danny La Rue International Spectacular, 93, 170-171
Danny La Rue Show, The, 93
Danvers, Billy, 41
Davies, Freddie, 154
Davis, Bette, 21, 37
de Carlo, Yvonne, 105
de la Tour, Frances, 141-145
de Leon, Jack, 176
Delfont, Bernard, 45, 101, 154, 172, 175
Derby, Crispin. 12, 13
Derek New Singers, The, 139, 171, 175
Devon, 12, 51, 58, 116, 164, 167
Dietrich, Marlene, 10, 21, 103, 129, 169
Diller, Phyllis, 21
Do a Good Turn When You Can, 38
Docker, Lady, 88, 163
Donnelly, Moya, 92
Dorchester Hotel, London, 46, 112
Dors, Diana, 88, 175

Drag (definition), 18
Drag, 158
Drag Queen Contests, 18
Driver, Betty, 77
Drury Lane Theatre, 34
Dublin, Ireland, 13, 157

EARNSHAW STREET, LONDON, 66
Ed Sullivan Show, 176
Edinburgh, 81
Edinburgh, Duke of, 125
Edward VII, King, 107
Edwards, Hilton, 157
Edwards, Miss, 54
Edwards, Sydney, 29, 119
Elizabeth II, Queen, 60, 101
Ellen, David, 93, 104, 139, 170, 176
Elstree, Herts, 152
Eltinge, Julian, 107-108
Emery, Dick, 22
Entertainer, The, 104
Escort Club, London, 74
Evening News, London, 153
Evening Standard, London, 29, 119
Everybody's Doing It, 165
Exeter, Devon, 51, 53, 54, 56, 61

'FANNY OAKLEY', 106
Farson, Daniel, 164-168
Felix, Julie, 91
Feydeau, Georges, 129, 174
Fields, Gracie, 132
Film Review, 9
Financial Times, 153
Fings Ain't Wot They Used T'be, 105
Finian's Rainbow, 176
First World War, 72, 76
Firth, Vincent, 9
Fisher, John, 155
Fitzgibbon, Maggie, 82-83, 163, 170
Fletcher, Cyril, 39
Fonteyn, Dame Margot, 37, 163
Forces in Petticoats, 71, 72
Forces Showboat, 70, 72, 75
Foresters, The, 34
Formby, George, 132
Fortnum and Mason, 176
France, 117, 132, 140-144, 160, 176
Frimley Green, Surrey, 41
Frost, David, 82, 105
Frost on Sunday, 102
Frost Report, The, 82
Funny Way to be a Hero, 155
Furse, Vanessa, 145

GABOR, ZSA ZSA, 178
Gallery First-Nighters, 42, 108
Gang Shows, 75-76
Gardiner, Mrs Doris, 163-164

Garland, Judy, 129
Gatty, Ted, 73-75, 77
Gay's the Word, 33
Genower, Peter, 110, 112
Gilbert and Sullivan, 34
Gilchrist, Roderick, 174
Gingold, Hermione, 21, 176
Girl Friend, The, 103
Globe Theatre, London, 34
Goddard, Mike, 170, 173, 176
Golders Green, London, 91
Goodbye Mr Chips, 93
Gordon, Leon, 59
Goring-on-Thames, Oxon, 116, 137
Grace, Princess, of Monaco, 18
Grand Order of Water Rats, 139, 175
Gray, Simon, 130
Grayson, Larry, 14-15, 41-44, 171
Great Russell Street, London, 66
Greece, 176
Green Dolphin, Blackpool, 172
Grosvenor House Hotel, London, 175
Guildford, Surrey, 105
Guinness, Sir Alec, 130
Guys and Dolls, 105

HAIR, 104
Hall, Stanley, 112-113
Hamlet, 128
Hampshire, 12
Hampstead, 58, 109, 117
Hanover Square Club (Danny La Rue's), 37, 38, 40, 42, 43, 45, 85, 92, 93, 104, 108, 157, 168, 172, 176
Hanson, Jack, 28, 117, 126, 138, 145-150, 168
Hart, Johnny, 176
Haslemere, Surrey, 122
Hatfield, Kristin, 145
Haymarket Theatre, London, 34
Haynes, Alan, 87, 91, 110, 170
Heath, Edward, 112
Heenan, Cardinal, 138
Hegmore Island, Berkshire, 116
Henie, Sonja, 84
Henley, Berkshire, 117, 137, 138
Hertfordshire, 145, 150, 152
Hildegarde, 21
Hill, Benny, 22
Hollywood, 160
Holman, Dennis, 122, 123, 172
Holt, Norfolk, 151
Home, William Douglas, 130
Hong Kong, 61
Hornsey Road, Blackpool, 172
Hotel de Paris, Cromer, Norfolk, 150
Hudd, Roy, 104, 170
Hulbert, Jack, 104, 176
Hullo Dolly, 118
Hunt, Jimmy, 145, 170

Hussein, King of Jordan, 18
Huttons (outfitters) Exeter, 53-57

I DID IT MY WAY, 154
Imperial Hotel, Blackpool, 134
Independent Television (ITV), 166
Invalid Children's Aid Association, 102
Ireland, 13, 50, 58, 157, 165
Irving Theatre, London, 73, 74, 76
Isolyn Gowns Ltd, 175
Italy, 112, 160

JACK THE RIPPER, 165
James, Jimmy, 166
Jameson, Rex, 75, 76-77
Japan, 60, 80, 128
Jesus Christ, Superstar, 160

KABUKI THEATRE OF JAPAN, 128
Karloff, Boris, 59
Kellett, Bob, 144
Kellor, Victor, 26-27
Kendall, Henry, 130
Kenn St Andrews Scout Group, 52-53
Kennford, Devon, 51-53, 55, 57, 58
Kensington, London, 127
Kensington Antiques Fair, 127
Kettner's Restaurant, Soho, London, 164
King Lear, 29
Kings Rhapsody, 104
Kiss Me Kate, 105

LADY BE GOOD, 29
'Lady Cynthia Grope', 80, 102, 106, 174
'Lady Godiva', 101
Lakeside Country Club, Frimley Green, 41
Lancashire, 12, 23, 93, 131-137, 169, 170, 172, 173, 175, 176
Landeau, Cecil, 73, 74
Las Vegas, 176
Lee, River, 50
Leicester Square, London, 73, 76, 159
Leonard, Hugh, 153
Leyland, Jenny, 170, 176
Liberace, 139-140
Lillie, Beatrice, 137
Lister, Moira, 105
Littlewood, Joan, 169
Lloyd, Marie, 76
London, 9, 10, 12, 13, 19, 23, 27, 32, 34, 36, 37, 38, 39, 42, 51, 55, 58, 61, 66, 70, 72, 76, 77, 85, 86, 87, 89, 90, 91, 92, 93, 104, 105, 107, 112, 131, 138, 143, 159, 160, 162, 163, 164, 165, 166, 171, 172, 175, 176
London Palladium, 47, 93, 101, 139, 162, 176
London School of Economics Students' Union, 127
London Weekend, 46, 154
Longford, Lord, 138-139

Los Angeles, 165
Los Diablos Del Bombo, 176, 178
Lowes, David, 92
Lukan, Mrs Agnes (*née* Goldsworthy), 54, 55-58
Lulu, 91
Lynn, Vera, 175

MACANDREW, PETER, 162-164
McCarthy, Adrian, 144-152
MacLiàmmóir, Michael, 156-157
Macmillan, Harold, 165
Mame, 118
Manchester, 41, 44, 74, 109, 175, 176
Mansfield, Jayne, 132
Margaret, HRH Princess, 37, 85, 102
Margate, Kent, 71, 88, 89
Marie Lloyd and Music Hall, 165, 166
Marks, Alfred, 141-144
Matthews, Sir Stanley, 132
Mayfair, London, 77
Mei Lan-Fang, 128-129
Melton Hall; Melton Constable, Norfolk, 150
Melville, Alan, 14, 33, 38-39
Men Only, 73, 74
Mermaid Theatre, London, 105
Miller, Max, 75, 123, 138, 158
Miller, Russell, 22, 72
Mills, John, 45-46
Mills, Richard M., 175
Misleading Ladies, 72
Miss TV Times Contest, 121-122
Miss World Beauty Contest, 121
'Mister Smith' – see Jim Wyatt
Mitchell, Una, 54, 55
Monroe, Marilyn, 23
Montreux Festival, 166
Moore, Bobby, 92
Moore, Roger, 121
Morecombe and Wise, 105
Moulin Rouge, 159
Mount, Peggy, 110
Mount Street, London, 89
Mountbatten, Earl, 121
Mousetrap, The, 41
'Mrs Shufflewick', see Rex Jameson
My Fair Lady, 159

NAPOLEON, 82
Nathans, see Bermans and Nathans
National Theatre, 29, 128
Neagle, Anna, 105, 132
'Nell Gwynne', 178
Nelson, Miss J. M., 66
New College of Speech and Drama, 69
New Reveille, 101, 122, 172
New Seekers, The, 154
New Theatre, Oxford, 109
Newcombe, Clovissa, 176
Nixon, David, 154-155

No, No, Nanette, 103, 105
Noel Coward Spectacular, 102
Norden, Denis, 122
Norfolk, 145, 150, 151
Northcott Theatre, Exeter, 61
Northen, Michael, 175, 176
Norwich, 26
Not in Front of the Children, 45
Novello, Ivor, 33, 34, 60, 86, 104
Nureyev, Rudolf, 37, 163

OAKES, PHILIP, 140
Observer, The, 10
O'Dea, Jimmy, 156
Ogilvy, Hon Mrs James, 175
Oh! What a Lovely War, 160, 169
Oh! You Beautiful Doll!, 166
Old MacDonald Had a Farm, 173
Old Vic Theatre, London, 176
Olivier, Sir Laurence, 9, 23, 104
On Mother Kelly's Doorstep, 91, 135, 173
Ondine, 176
Opera House, Blackpool, 170-171
Op-timists, The, 103
O'Reilly, Miss, 54
Oslo, Norway, 13, 90
Our Miss Fred, 46-47, 102, 131, 132, 140-154, 159, 161
Oxford, 40, 109
Oxford, Michael C., 117
Oxford Street, London, 66, 73

PAIGE, JANIS, 118
Paignton, Devon, 42
Palace Theatre, London, 45, 102, 103-107, 109
Palace Theatre, Manchester, 109
Palace Theatre of Varieties, 103
Palmer, Toni, 104-105, 123, 134, 135, 170
Panshanger, Herts, 152
Panton Street, London, 112
Patton, 160
Pavlova, 103
Payne, Mr and Mrs, 54, 55
Peel, Lady, see Beatrice Lillie
Percival, Lance, 141-144
Peter Pan, 131
Phillips, Leslie, 46
Pontings Holiday Camp, Blackpool, 172
Powell, Dilys, 153
Prime of Miss Jean Brodie, The, 159-160
Prince and the Showgirl, The, 23
Prince of Wales theatre, London, 9, 13, 93, 171, 173, 178
Private Eye, 139
Pyjama Tops, 37

Q THEATRE, 176
Queen Mary Hall, London, 69
Queen of Hearts, 75, 87, 109-112, 176

Queen Passionella and The Sleeping Beauty, 89, 91-93, 105
Queen's Theatre, Blackpool, 172
Queen's Theatre, London, 72

RAG TRADE, THE, 105
Rainier, Prince of Monaco, 18
Ratcliffe, Jim, 53
Ratcliffe, Mrs Honor (née Preece), 52-53
Reader, Ralph, 75-76
Redman, Lister, 135
Reeves, Mrs Peggy, 53-55
Regents Park, London, 164
René, Ricky, 169
Revaudeville, 32
Raymond, Paul, 42
Richmond, Surrey, 66
Rise Above It, 176
Ritz Hotel, London, 82
Rix, Brian, 89, 129
Robinson, David, 153
Rogers, Ginger, 171
Romeo and Juliet, 59
Rosse, Countess of, 37
Royal Academy of Music, 69
Royal Air Force, 75, 76, 81, 141, 159
Royal Albert Hall, London, 75
Royal Ballet, 176
Royal Command Shows, 45, 75, 93, 101, 103, 139, 140, 176
Royal English Opera House, 103
Royal Navy, 58-59, 60, 61
Royal Opera House, 176
Royal Television Show, 91
Russell Harty Plus, 154
Ryan's Daughter, 160

SABRINA, 88
Salute to the Stars, 139
Sands, Jackie, 89, 92, 101, 104
Saville Theatre, London, 89
Savoy Hotel, London, 45, 121
Schofield, Paul, 18
Scotland, 93
Secombe, Harry, 71
Secombe, Jenny, 71
Second World War, 51, 52, 54, 56, 72, 75, 76, 159
Shaftesbury Avenue, London, 72
Shakespeare, 29, 59, 104, 128, 174, 176
Shaw, Sandie, 91, 172, 173
Shaw, Tommy, 175
Shoreham, Sussex, 93, 117
Showboat Express, 72
Showbusiness Personality of the Year, 45, 102, 175
Shut That Door, 41
Simond, Mrs Pauline, 66-69
Sinatra, Frank, 10, 23, 145

Singapore, 58-59, 61
Sleeping Beauty, The, 91
Slinger, Gerry, 23, 47-48
Smith, Dodie, 67
Snowdon, Lord, 37, 85, 102, 103, 108, 175
Soho, London, 164
Soldiers in Skirts, 70, 72
Solly, Bill, 105
Sound of Music, The, 91
South Africa, 105
Southport, Lancs, 169
Spain, 160
Spinetti, Victor, 77, 84-86, 170
Splinters, 72, 76
Squires, Dorothy, 171
Stage, The, 10, 134, 154, 172
Starr, Ringo, 37
Stars of the Year, 154
Stars Organisation for Spastics, 174, 175
Stewart, Pauline, see Mrs Pauline Simond
Stoll Theatre, London, 76
Stork Room, London, 42
Stratford, East London, 86
Sultan of Morocco, The, 165
Sun, The, 153
Sunday Times, 140, 153
Surrey, 122
Sussex, 12, 117, 152
Sutcliffe, Berkeley, 175-176
Swan Inn, Streatley, Berks, 112, 116, 139, 157

TALBOT, MARY, 89-90
Taliday, Miss, 54
Talk of the Town, 104
Taylor, Elizabeth, 88, 92, 178
Television Personality of the Year, 45
Tempest, Marie, 103
Thames TV, 121-122
Thatched Barn, The, Barnet, 152
Theatre Personality of the Year, 108
Theatre Royal, Exeter, 61
These Are The Days, 38
This is Your Life, 14, 44
This Week, 165
Thomas, Brandon, 46
Thomas, Caitlin, 165
Those Good Old, Bad Old Days, 172
Tingley, Cynthia, 162
Tipthorp, Peter, 45, 50-51, 90, 117, 123
Tokyo, 60
Tommy Shaw Dancers, 139, 171, 175
Tondelayo, 59
Toulouse-Lautrec, 82
Trafford Gallery, London, 89
Trehill, Kenn, Devon, 52
Trueman, Freddie, 93
TV Times, 110, 118, 122
Twang, 82

Twigge, Jenny, 145
Twiggy, 140

VAL DOONICAN SHOW, THE, 176
Van Damm, Vivian, 32, 33
Variety Club of Great Britain, 45, 46, 102, 112, 121, 125, 139, 174
Vidrobes Ltd, 35
Vivat! Vivat! Regina!, 160
Vogue, 108
Vosburgh, Dick, 105

WALDRON, JOHN R., 52-53
Walker, Billy, 92
Wallbank, Linda, 136
Wallbank, Raymond, 133-136
Wansey-Jackson, Carla, 122
Ward, Barry, 154
Wattis, Richard, 39-40, 89, 170
Way of the World, The, 130
Wells, Billy, 75
West, Mae, 21, 84, 126, 169, 171, 178
Weyland Hospital, Bradfield, Berks, 125
What's a Girl Like You, 46
Where's Charley?, 104
Whipton, near Exeter, Devon, 53
White Cargo, 59
Whitehall Theatre, 34, 37, 89

Whitehouse, Mary, 139
Williams, Charlie, 154
Williams, Tennessee, 93
Willis, Lord 'Ted', 46-47, 153
Wilson, Colin, 165
Wilson, Seretta, 145
Windmill Theatre, 32-33, 76, 93
Windsor, Barbara, 85, 89, 170
Windsor Castle, 107
Winstons Club, 74, 81, 82, 83, 84, 86, 90, 163, 165
Wisdom, Norman, 104, 153
Wise Child, 130
Wogan, Terry, 26-27
Wood, George ('Wee Georgie Wood'), 156
Wolfe, Digby, 82
Women's Royal Voluntary Service, 126
Wyatt, Jim, 74
Wyfold, Reading, Berks, 125
Wynne, Edmund E., 134, 136, 137
Wynne, Hon. Mrs, 136

YOUNG GENERATION BIG TOP, 172
Young Men's Christian Association, 66, 67
Young Winston, 160
Young Women's Christian Association, 15, 66, 67, 68, 69
Yvonne Arnauld Theatre, Guildford, 105